IN
VENEZUELA

IN
VENEZUELA

Michael Palin

HUTCHINSON
HEINEMANN

CONTENTS

Introduction   1

Map   4

IN VENEZUELA   7

Postscript   179

Chronology   182

Acknowledgements   185

THERE IS SOMETHING ABOUT THE NAME VENEZUELA.
It has a ring to it. It trips enticingly off the tongue. It sounds exotic, tropical, ever so slightly unreal. An author would be pleased to have thought of it. A billionaire would nod approvingly as it was painted on the bow of his yacht. Indulgent parents would regret their daughter shortening it to Venny.

It's a restaurant you wouldn't mind being seen coming out of, or a nightclub you wouldn't mind being seen going into. It could be the name of a saint or a female pirate. A cocktail or a luxury hammock.

Such thoughts crossed my mind when I decided to make it my hundredth country to visit. I'm glad to have been to Egypt and Moldova, to Iraq and Mali, but none has the same alluring cadence as Ven-Ez-Ue-La.

So hallucinatory is the name, indeed, that even after my trip I'm still not sure I've actually been there. It's home to the tallest waterfall and the highest cable car in the world, to desert and snow, to mighty anacondas and exotic blue crabs, and I know for a fact that I have seen them all. But somehow, because they're all wrapped up in the magic word 'Venezuela', they don't seem quite real. I'm also acutely aware that, seasoned traveller though I am, until we actually arrived in Venezuela I had no idea of what to expect or what to prepare myself for.

But that's what made those three weeks on the road so unusually exciting.

There would have been a time, some fifty years ago, when everyone would have been talking about Venezuela. It was an oil-boom success story, an investor's dream, a steadfast friend of its powerful neighbour across the Caribbean. It was the USA of South America.

And then in 1998, an army officer called Hugo Chávez turned this relationship on its head. Chávez was a friend of the people. The Venezuelan people, not the American people. He was a bit of Guevara and a bit of Castro. He had a big smile and punched the air a lot. After he came to power the image of Venezuela as a comfortable capitalist haven was replaced by that of a purposeful disruptor of the status quo as Chávez nationalised key industries, revolutionised social and welfare programmes and sought new friends on the international stage.

The oil money kept coming in, but now much of the profit it generated, rather than flowing to Wall Street, was directed by the president to the poorest in his own country – those who had previously failed to benefit from the wealth it created. Venezuela might, in the process, have become an inspiration to many, but it also alienated its richer citizens, and – crucially – its former ally to the north.

By the time that Chávez died of cancer in 2013 at the age of fifty-eight, his socialist dream was already fading. Spiralling government spending had caused the national debt to increase sixfold. Inflation

had reached record levels. Oil revenues had fallen. His successor, Nicolás Maduro, lacking Chávez's powerful charisma, turned increasingly to the police and the army to enforce his will, and they proceeded to help him win three terms of office, each more authoritarian than the last. At his latest inauguration, a month before we set out on our journey in early February 2025, Maduro had become, to all intents and purposes, a dictator.

I have always been attracted to countries whose problems seem to outweigh their potential. Along with the team led by my director and series producer Neil Ferguson, I'd visited North Korea, Iraq and Nigeria to see how they were coping. Venezuela may have sounded more laid-back and more appealing than all of them, but what I found was that despite its beauty and bountiful resources the country was not living up to its promise.

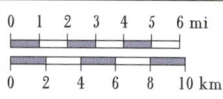

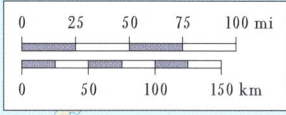

ARRIVAL

IT'S LATE AFTERNOON WHEN THE COAST OF VENEZUELA comes into sight. There's something epic about seeing land after flying over ocean for so long. How much greater must have been the satisfaction for Christopher Columbus when he first glimpsed this same coastline on his third voyage from Europe after weeks at sea.

When he and his crew finally made landfall on what is now Venezuela's Paria Peninsula on 5th August 1498, Columbus thought he had landed on an island. In fact the land on which he and his men first stepped stretched southwards for almost 5,000 miles. They were the first Europeans to set foot in South America.

It took them several weeks to cross the Atlantic, and here I am feeling impatient that we have been in the sky for nine hours.

The Venezuelan coast grows closer, and more impressive. The blur on the horizon slowly becomes defined as a long range of mountains, plunging sheer into the sea. The sun is setting behind them, sending their jagged shadows across the surface of the ocean. Though we're descending fast I can see nowhere to land.

The man in the seat in front of me is unmoved. He is much more absorbed in episodes of *Friends*, which he's been watching for the last few hours. He loves them. His regular, rich gurgles of laughter could have been irritating, but somehow they become infectious, and I find myself laughing at his laughter. A reassuring alternative to the endless liturgy of flight announcements.

We have turned now and are running eastwards, parallel to the steep coastline. A few small beaches are tucked at the base of the mountains. Patches of smoke rise from thick forest. These give way to settlements and an industrial plant and finally, and rather reassuringly, a wider cleared area broad enough for us to land.

Touching down in a country new to me is always an excitement, multiplied this time by this being the one hundredth I've visited. But there's an added touch of mystery to this adventure as conventional guidebooks to Venezuela have been so hard to come by. The best I could find was a second-hand Lonely Planet from 2010, remaindered by the Borough of Poole Library. I came across a more up-to-date assessment of the country in a 2024 publication called *Venezuela's Collapse: The Long Story of How Things Fell Apart*, but the present government don't take kindly to criticism so I wasn't encouraged to bring that. In fact I was advised, as we all were, to bring the minimum of printed material about our trip. Venezuela is without many friends in the West. Only a handful of European carriers – such as Iberia, TAP and Europa – fly directly to Caracas. The Turkish Airlines flight to Cuba makes a stop here.

Looking around as we exit the plane everything seems muted. I count four other aircraft parked up at jetties, none of them airlines I recognise, and there are few other people inside the customs and immigration areas. On the walls of the terminal are likenesses of President Maduro, posters encouraging informers, and most bizarrely, an old-style notice headed *'Se Busca'* (wanted) with a black-and-white photo of Edmundo González Urrutia. He was the man who stood against Nicolás Maduro in last year's election and who was deemed by a careful examination of votes cast to have defeated him quite conclusively. But Maduro

declared himself the winner for a third term, and González was forced to seek refuge abroad. Hence the *'Se Busca'* notices offering a $100,000 reward for information leading to his capture. About two weeks before we arrived Donald Trump raised the reward for the capture of González's nemesis Maduro to $25 million. It's very much tit for tat.

All this leaves a chill feeling in the air, as does the long delay while our credentials are checked by officials in loose-fitting grey cotton uniforms. Most are inscrutable. A few seem friendly. But none of them has the authority to let us enter the country. This rests with some nameless figure who 'will come soon'. Three and a half inexplicable hours later we are allowed to progress through immigration. By the

time we rendezvous with our fixer Freddy and his team of drivers, the only things we want to see in Venezuela are hotel beds.

The drive from the airport into the capital, Caracas, shows another side of the country. A state-of-the-art *autopista* winds its way through the mountains, along well-lit roads and through tunnels that are often colourfully decorated with tiles or murals. It all seems rather more welcoming than the grey officialdom at the airport. We head into the busy cluster of buildings at the heart of this four-hundred-year-old city. It resembles any other Western capital, apart from the presence of massive billboards bearing the square, unlined, almost baby-like face of President Maduro.

I DRAW BACK MY CURTAINS AND TAKE MY FIRST LOOK at the Venezuelan capital in daylight. I'm on the twenty-fourth floor of the Renaissance hotel. Around me are equally tall tower blocks. What makes this such an impressive view, however, is not the city below me but the mountains above. Caracas, set in a valley, is dwarfed by the green-clad range of the Parque Nacional El Ávila, which protects the city from the sea.

Our hotel is in the upscale neighbourhood of Chacao. Even so, I'm still warned not to go out on my own. I'm already learning that what you see is not quite what you get in Venezuela.

When we arrived yesterday, we discovered that various bits of kit had not been put on the plane in Madrid. The crew are therefore having to improvise frantically. With a bit of ingenuity, and a lot of help from our Venezuelan assistant producer Emiliana (or 'Em', as she's generally known), we are able to assemble enough equipment to start work.

I'm introduced to Caracas by Ana, a lively, talkative local who, as a correspondent for an American newspaper, wrote a front-page story about the controversial 2024 election, which Maduro claimed to have won even though Edmundo González secured more votes. No one has been able to dislodge Maduro, and so for a further six years he will continue to be the voice and face of his country. According to Ana, though, things were arguably even worse a decade ago. Then hyper-inflation, which Maduro wholly failed to address, rendered the national

currency – the bolívar – virtually worthless. In the ensuing economic crisis, some seven million Venezuelans left the country to seek new lives abroad. Given that the population numbered barely thirty million at the time, that mass exodus left a big hole in the economy. Should she be telling me all this? I wonder. She smiles. Not only is Chacao, where we are now, an affluent neighbourhood, it's also strongly opposed to the current government. Ana knows that she is unlikely to face any hostility from passers-by.

In any case, there's little sense of political crisis as we walk around Chacao, or when we take the clean, efficient Caracas metro across town to La Hoyada, a popular street market. Here there are more murals on the walls than there are policemen on the beat. It's eye-catching art, often inspired by religious images (the country is

predominantly Catholic), always decorated with brightly coloured and abstract patterns. The sun is strong, but because of where the city lies in the mountains, the heat is dry and bearable. People shout *'Gringo!'* (foreigner) at me – derisively if they think I'm American, more warmly when they learn that I'm from the UK.

But we can't escape politics altogether. Ana explains that the wall posters I've noticed amid the murals are calls to arms, urging people to back the government in its claims on territory on its eastern border with Guyana. Essequibo, as the disputed slice of Guyana is called, has been revealed to have substantial oil reserves, and in 2024 the Maduro government passed a law making it a new state of Venezuela. The UK, US and Brazil all opposed this land grab.

With these various issues swirling about, I ask Ana how challenging life is for a journalist in Venezuela today, and what it's like to live here.

'I see it as a very beautiful, interesting place,' she replies, 'filled with chaos.'

In the cool of the evening, I find myself away from the crowds and the chaos, in a small tree-shaded plaza dominated by a statue of the greatest Venezuelan of them all, Simón Bolívar. Born Simón José Antonio de la Santísima Trinidad Bolívar y Palacios Ponte y Blanco, into a wealthy Caracas family, he was educated abroad where he acquired the values of the Enlightenment and, returning to Caracas, proceeded to lead the fight for Venezuelan independence against Royalist Spanish forces. Bolívar was a larger-than-life character. His leadership skills were legendary. So was his appetite, not just for battle, but for food, dance, music and ladies.

He is known and revered as El Libertador – the Liberator – who almost single-handedly took on the armies of the Spanish crown,

and drew the map of much of modern South America in the process. Besides Venezuela he created present-day Colombia, Peru and Bolivia.

This fine equestrian statue has Bolívar, his cloak spread behind him, astride a majestically rearing horse. The inscription translates simply as, '*Born in Caracas 24th July 1783. Died in Santa Marta 17th December 1830.*'

Though he was still in his forties when he died his legacy is inescapable. The airport is named after him, the currency is named after him, and when Hugo Chávez won power in 1999, he took the Liberator's mantle, calling his socialist programme the Bolívarian Revolution and re-naming his country the Bolívarian Republic of Venezuela.

The small square with its four fountains is peaceful and well looked after. The only jarring note is a strident whistle blown by the park keeper when any of the children clamber onto the base of Bolívar's statue.

Back at the hotel we celebrate the end of our first full day in the city with Polar beer, a local pilsner that is both refreshing and in such small bottles that we soon have a row of them down the table.

Jet lag will probably confuse my sleep pattern, but before I turn out the light I read a few more pages of *The General in His Labyrinth*, Gabriel García Márquez's wonderful novel about the last days of who else but Simón Bolívar.

✦✦DAY✦
3

CARACAS

ON OUR WAY IN FROM THE AIRPORT WE PASSED BY mountain slopes covered in twinkling lights. By day we can see that these were lights from the many *barrios* that cover the mountainsides – improvised accommodation originally built to house the workers drawn to Caracas in the oil-led economic boom of the 1950s, '60s and early '70s.

Today we're on our way to Petare, east of Caracas, above which, stretching up the mountains, is one of the largest of these *barrios*.

It has been difficult to get permission to film here. These slums harbour some of the criminal gangs which once earned Caracas the title of Most Dangerous City in the World, and we have had to work hard to

build trust within the community. As we turn in off the busy main road, we find ourselves, to my surprise, in a sunny square, surrounded on all sides by freshly painted, brightly coloured single-storey period houses, and by the big shady trees that are such a feature of the city. In the centre of the square, beside the national flag, is another triumphal equestrian statue, for once not bearing the name of Bolívar, but that of Antonio José de Sucre, his friend and fellow liberator.

It turns out that many of the houses have been done up by the various NGOs that are working to improve conditions in the *barrio*. They are appealing to a sense of history by calling their programme '400 Years of Petare 1621 to 2021'.

I'm introduced to Katiuska Camargo, a woman of great warmth, known to all as Kati. She's been a community worker in Petare for years and knows these narrow streets well. Her upbeat positivity dispels any fears I might have had about the filming here. She works hard and I can tell she's a great motivator. She would like to see more women in Venezuelan politics and twinkles with coyness when I ask about her own ambitions. Would she like to be president one day? Her smile broadens, leaving me in no doubt as to the answer.

She talks a lot about community spirit, of trying to involve people in the simple things of everyday life: looking after their streets, clearing litter, painting murals, getting to know their neighbours. As she takes me up the hill further into the *barrio*, it becomes clear that she practises what she preaches. Everyone seems to know her and trust her, and she has a big smile and a greeting for them all.

But there's someone she'd especially like me to meet.

Following her up some precariously improvised steps that zigzag upwards off the street, I feel my way carefully, amazed at how jumbled these houses are, built on top of and against each other in an unplanned maze. Eventually we reach a doorway at which we're greeted by a woman who must be about Kati's age. She's called Yaya, and she invites us into her tiny but well-furnished three-roomed home. Inside there's scarcely space to move.

A little boy hides shyly behind her. His name is Aleph and he's three years old.

Yaya is not his mother but his auntie. Such has been the struggle to make a living in Venezuela since the disastrous recent years of hyperinflation that his real mother, Yasenia – Yaya's sister – decided to leave the country, and take the refugee trail up through the Darién Gap and eventually to the USA.

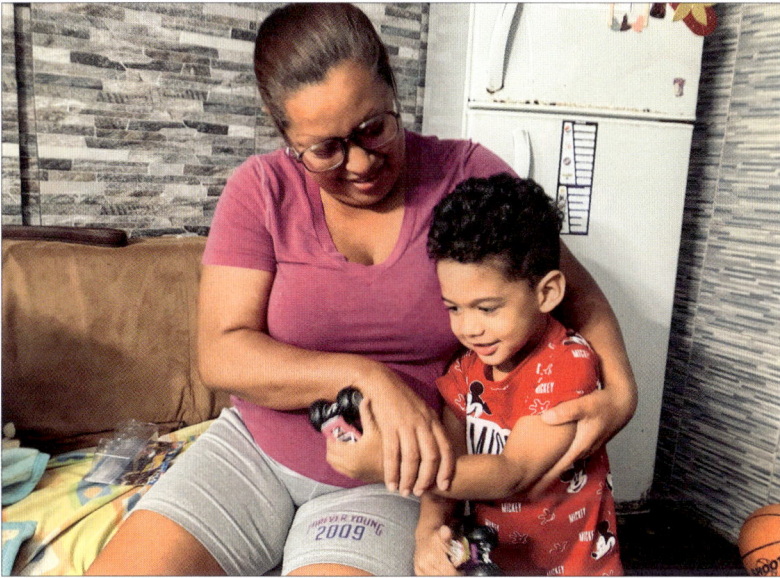

At first, I learn, Yasenia was determined to take her son with her, but Yaya sought to dissuade her, for the route through the Darién Gap is fearfully difficult and dangerous. In the end they agreed that she would go, but that Aleph would stay here with his auntie. Yasenia then set out, made her way through the Gap and finally arrived in Florida.

That was two years ago, and the family remains split. While we were there his mother rang, as she does every day. She sounded cheerful and made her son laugh, but there was no talk of reunion, and I felt, as she wound up the call, that the two might never see each other again.

We retrace our steps to the entrance of the *barrio*, buzzed all along the way by motor scooters. They're everywhere in Caracas, and are never driven at less than full speed as they hurtle through traffic, hooting shrilly, swerving suicidally. As our driver and fixer Freddy says, shaking his head, 'They don't have brakes. They have horns.'

Everywhere you go in Caracas you see walls, bridges and billboards festooned with the face of the nation's founder, Simón Bolívar, and, beside him, the charismatic army officer who led his country for fourteen years, Hugo Chávez. The coming together of the two great names in Venezuelan history is realised in the spectacular Bolívar Mausoleum.

Previously, Bolívar's remains had lain alongside other great national heroes in the National Pantheon, but when Chávez became president he had Bolívar's body exhumed to ascertain whether a longstanding rumour that the Liberator had been poisoned was true or false. No evidence of poison was discovered, but rather than re-inter the remains in the Pantheon, Chávez decided his hero should have his own resting place nearby. The dramatic, soaring sailboat design cost $90 million. It towers 177 feet (54 metres) over the National Pantheon below. At the time it was considered to be a memorial more to Chávez's ego than Bolívar's achievements.

It is one of the great landmark buildings of Caracas and we were looking forward to filming inside. However, permission was revoked at the last minute and without explanation. Earlier that day, our second unit was temporarily detained and then cautioned for filming outside another government building. The two experiences have added to the uncomfortable feeling that an eye is being kept on us.

It's therefore quite a relief that we are covering nothing more controversial this evening than a Valentine's night celebration in the foothills to the east of Caracas. The place to party is the picture-book town of El Hatillo (Little Ranch). It could hardly be more different from the *barrio* of Petare. El Hatillo is an attractive, well-heeled neighbourhood that's become a much-favoured getaway from the noise and stress of the city centre.

The trouble is that so popular is Valentine's night in El Hatillo that a stream of vehicles clogs the approach roads, perfectly recreating the noise and stress they're trying to get away from.

My companion for the evening is called, appropriately, Valentina. She's a television star who has made a highly successful series of documentaries about her travels around Venezuela. I reckon I might learn a thing or two from her.

I meet her beneath a heart-shaped arch of red balloons at the entrance to a cobbled street, lined with period houses, which stretches up the hill. Today it's closed to traffic. It has also been appropriately decorated for the occasion. Those who've booked sit expectantly at tables with red tops, candles and bottles of wine. On a temporary stage, music thumps away and a fine young violinist brings Queen's 'Bohemian Rhapsody' to life.

Valentina Quintero, for whom the word 'vivacious' could have been coined, is seventy going on nineteen. She has a mass of curly blonde

hair, sports big red-framed glasses, and is wearing bright red trousers to complement her white blouse. As we walk up the street to our table she's greeted with respectful nods by those who have bought tickets and wide-eyed enthusiasm by those who haven't. I stand to one side, savouring my anonymity, as she signs autographs and poses for selfies.

Her age and celebrity have given her a freedom to talk openly about the situation in the country. She acknowledges that things are far from perfect and that a lot of talented people have fled Venezuela in the last decade. But she herself would never leave the country. 'We decided, about four years ago, that we cannot take the dictatorship out . . . and we are going to stay, because we love the country.' As with many Venezuelans I've met so far, laughter is important to her – even laughter about political topics. 'We can get through this dictatorship because of the sense of humour.' Food, it rapidly becomes apparent, is important too. When *tequeños* – cheese sticks inside fried dough – arrive, Valentina pushes them across to me while simultaneously rhapsodising about what treats are still to come.

As we eat, we talk about her travel documentaries. 'I wanted people from Venezuela to know Venezuela,' she says, simply. When I tell her what I'm hoping to see, her responses fill me with infectious enthusiasm.

'You're going to see how different it is everywhere you go.' To which she adds, 'Always be looking out of the window.'

DAY 4

CARACAS

VENEZUELA'S RULERS HAVE ALWAYS REVELLED IN THE grand gesture. And the discovery of oil in the early twentieth century, which for a while made the country one of the wealthiest in the world, provided plenty of opportunities for its leaders to do so. President Marcos Pérez Jiménez, the army officer who ran Venezuela for much of the 1950s, is a case in point. Before he was deposed by a popular uprising in 1958, he decided that quite a lot of the nation's wealth should be spent on a world-class hotel. In Caracas itself? No, that would be too easy. How about on top of a mountain? Accessed by a dedicated cable-car lift which would carry guests up to their accommodation nearly 6,500 feet (2,000 metres) above the capital?

Amazingly, this project was realised and the Humboldt hotel opened to the public in 1956. Less amazingly, it closed four years later.

Today, in one of Maduro's grand gestures, the fourteen-storey mountain-top hotel has been reopened after a substantial facelift. I therefore elect to join the queue to board one of the gondolas that will take me up to the Pico El Ávila, the highest point of the range of mountains separating Caracas from the sea, in order to visit it.

It's a holiday weekend and the lifts are full of families taking picnics up to the mountain top and hoping that the cloud will lift sufficiently for them to take in the spectacular view of Caracas on one side and the blue Caribbean on the other. We have lunch at a small, busy eatery that serves the ubiquitous *arepas* – corn pancakes stuffed with an apparently limitless variety of fillings – and pulled-pork sandwiches, known as *sánduches de Pernil*. Venezuelans don't hold back on the portions and I find my heavily stuffed sandwich impossible to eat gracefully.

Every now and then golf buggies carrying more affluent customers the half-mile to the hotel make their way through the make-shift cluster of stalls and snack bars. We follow them, past a security gate and up to the entrance of the hotel. A strikingly bold column of steel and glass, the Humboldt looks as if it's been plucked from some urban business district. Beneath the porte cochère, doormen step forward to open car doors and unload bags. The hotel is busy this weekend, despite its lofty inaccessibility.

The big surprise is how chic it is inside. The architecture makes the most of the light pouring in on all sides and the interior design is breathtaking. There is much creative use of glass, wood and copper. Thought – and money – has gone into recreating the furnishing and fabrics of the modernist style of the 1950s and '60s. All in all it's one of the most remarkable hotels I've ever seen.

It seems out on a limb, a sort of impossible dream, but it's clearly well looked after. Apparently President Maduro uses it for entertaining. So maybe the socialist future of Venezuela is decided in this luxury eyrie.

Back in my downtown hotel I watch some of Maduro's three-hour-long weekly television show – the successor to Hugo Chávez's *Aló Presidente* broadcast which ran, unscripted, for several hours every Sunday morning. Chávez made very effective use of television to talk at great length to his people. Maduro is a less impressive performer. Accompanied by his wife, he talks on and on at his various guests about everything. At one unguarded moment he refers to his inauguration with surely mistaken candidness. 'One month ago I swore myself into power,' he appears to say, before dismissing the subject with an unconvincing laugh. No one seems to notice. By the time the three hours are up, the father of the country is clearly exhausted. When the final music plays he rouses himself to dance with all sorts of people in strange costumes. It's very bizarre.

★DAY★
5

CARACAS TO CANAIMA

IT'S THE CARACAS MARATHON TODAY, AND MANY ROADS
will be closed from 5 a.m., so we have to leave the Renaissance hotel
well before dawn for our 7.30 flight south towards the Amazon. Our
destination is the small town of Canaima, the gateway to a huge
national park. Covering 12,000 square miles, the park is the sixth-
largest in the world, and contains among other things the Angel Falls,
the tallest waterfall on the planet.

Our plane is a Brazilian-built Embraer 190, and our flight is one
of only two large-scale ones to Canaima scheduled each week. Though
I have my precious copy of García Márquez's novel about the last days
of Simón Bolívar to read, my eye is irresistibly drawn to the in-flight
magazine. It's called *Presidencia* and is totally devoted to Bolívar's

latest successor. On the cover is a mocked-up photo of Maduro, Xi Jinping and Vladimir Putin standing side by side. Inside, Maduro's likeness is on every page, greeting foreign visitors, helmeted in a steelworks, arm around the shoulder of an elderly citizen. His bland, smooth-skinned face has only one distinguishing feature, a thick black moustache. With nothing much else to go on, his publicity team have made the most of this, turning Maduro into a Superman-style caped crusader called Super Bigote – Super Moustache. The magazine carries a six-page cartoon strip of Super Bigote graphically punching out his rivals. Edmundo González is seen drinking whisky with an evil-looking Uncle Sam, while opposition leader María Corina Machado, teeth bared, is depicted as a shrieking, drooling witch.

I check the date of the magazine. It's from October 2024, around two months after the controversial re-election of Maduro for a third term. One hears a lot about dignity in defeat. These images show a desperate lack of dignity in victory.

We head south-east on the seven-hundred-mile flight to Canaima. As the minutes tick by, the sheer size of the country is brought home to me. It's as big as France and Spain put together. A green carpet of jungle and rainforest spreads beneath us, broken only by flashes of sunlight reflected off the Orinoco river and its tributaries. Rising in Colombia and disgorging 1,300 miles (2,100 kilometres) later in a huge sprawling delta on Venezuela's Atlantic coast, the Orinoco is one of the great rivers of South America.

As we descend into Canaima I catch my first glimpse of one of the most characteristic sights of the region they call La Gran Sabana. Rising here and there above the dense surrounding rainforest are massive tables of rock known as *tepuis*. Flat-topped and majestic, they look like

colossal medieval castles. In fact they are the lone remains of a sand-stone plateau, the Guyana Shield, that once covered the area. It is one of the oldest geological features in the world. Protected by inaccessibly sheer-sided walls, the *tepuis* have evolved their own ecosystems, which continue to fascinate scientists and adventurers. The tallest of them, Roraima, over 9,000 feet (nearly 3,000 metres) high, was the inspiration for Sir Arthur Conan Doyle's classic novel *The Lost World*.

The Canaima National Park is in the land of the Pemon people, an indigenous group who were living a nomadic existence in south-eastern Venezuela long before the Spanish arrived. Thanks to Chávez, who was keen to acknowledge the rights of the pre-Hispanic peoples of his country, they now own and administer the national park. We first encounter them as they check our passports at the airstrip. A wedding group from Caracas, who have just spent the weekend there, will take our plane back. Other than that, it's very quiet.

The airport buildings may be thatched and their setting distinctly pastoral, but there are still careful customs checks to be gone through

and a tourist tax to pay before we can climb into the backs of trucks and be driven slowly and bumpily through the village to Waku Lodge, our home for the next two nights.

Its location takes the breath away. The straw-roofed, open-sided public areas slope down through a well-kept garden to the shores of a lagoon, fed, on the far side, by a series of thunderous waterfalls. Their roar, though muted by a half-mile distance, is the constant soundtrack to this Eden-like spot.

Later that day, I'm to get to know one of them more intimately. Arturo, a broad-shouldered Pemon with a big, reassuring face, takes me

out across the water to the widest and fullest of the waterfalls, behind which it's possible to walk. As a pensioner, two months away from my eighty-second birthday, I'm constantly warned about slippery pavements, so there's a sort of exhilaration to being encouraged so thoroughly to break the rules. Clambering up a rocky path I come to the entry point, beyond which a wall of water thumps and crashes. The way behind this deluge is across a series of wet, irregular stones and through an unavoidable gateway of water, which resembles a plastic strip curtain at the back of a shop.

There are no guard rails, no health and safety warnings. Though I'm offered a supportive arm across the stones, I realise I have to do this for myself. Nervously praying that my balance will be steady l set out, picking my way ever so gingerly over the stones, through a cold shower of water and finally into a chamber of jagged rocks and roaring water.

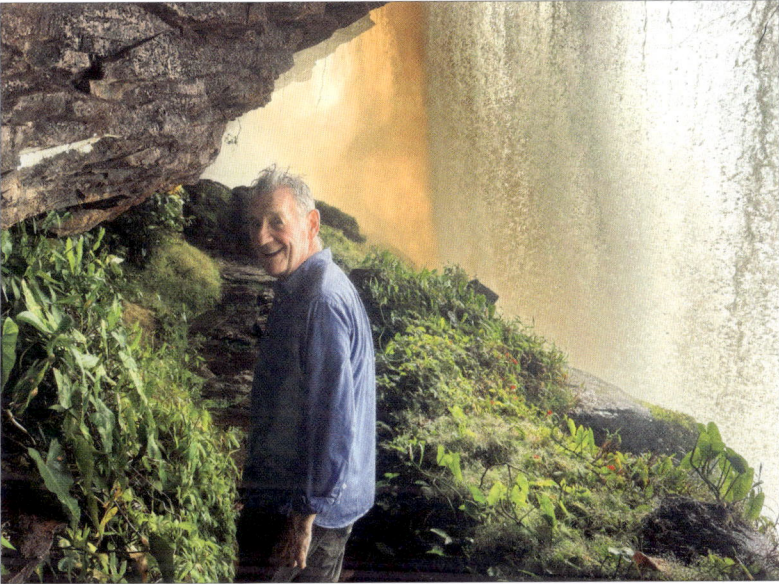

Blown spray douses me.

Standing, not entirely securely, on shiny black rock only feet away from a wall of water powerful enough to crush me to pieces, I'm gripped by a combination of excitement and sheer terror. I feel an irresistible urge to shout at the top of my voice. Then, just as I'm in the midst of my raving, I spot a young couple, bent double, picking their way along the path towards me. Almost unbelievably, the father is clutching an infant, who can't be more than five. As the water crashes around us I feel a strange connection with that small child. The two of us, at opposite ends of life, doing a very silly thing. Brought together amid the implacable force of nature, there's nothing either of us can do but freeze, in fear and wonder.

Such is my sense of elation that after I've got back to the lodge and dried out, I have to have two gin and tonics to bring me down to earth.

Later, as I head for bed, along the trail to my cabin, I can hear the continuous roar of the falls across the lagoon. Somewhere in my mind comes the thought that they ought to be switched off at night. Then, of course, I realise that they are more than just a tourist attraction. The water that thundered past me this afternoon has been falling every second of every day and every night for hundreds of thousands of years.

I sleep like a baby until the dawn chorus of toucans, macaws and parrots reminds me that I've left Caracas well behind.

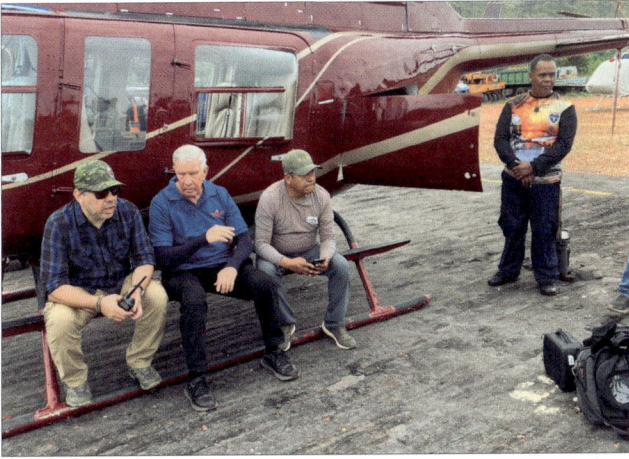

CANAIMA

NO REST FOR THE WICKED. TODAY THERE ARE OTHER watery challenges to face. We are out at the airstrip early to pack and board a helicopter which, we hope, will land us at the base of the Angel Falls, the tallest free fall of water in the world.

As Jaimie on camera and Joe on sound load themselves up with all the kit they will need for the day's work, our pilot, Freddy, sits quietly as we are given a safety briefing. He must be in his sixties. He has a shock of white hair and bears an uncomfortable resemblance to *Airplane!* star Leslie Nielsen.

Unfortunately, the weather conditions are not in our favour. The falls are reported to be obscured by cloud, which we can only hope may clear as the day goes on. But we take off anyway, to see for ourselves.

It's not long before we find that there are other problems out there more serious than a lack of visibility.

In amongst the uniform green cover below us are odd treeless patches of white and brown, looking from the air like sore spots where the green cover has been scratched away. Our fixer, Freddy, tells me that these are the result of illegal gold mining, which is becoming an increasing threat. Environmental groups have identified over thirty such sites in the national park.

We put down to take a closer look at one of them. The contrast with the rainforest around is striking and depressing. To find gold the natural cover has first to be stripped away to get at the sand beneath. This then has to be leached with mercury to free the gold from the sand. The result is a wasteland.

Shorn of tree cover, the area is exposed to the full heat of a powerful midday sun. Without vegetation to absorb the moisture the air is unbearably humid. Yet even so, there are a handful of people digging away, leaving a trail of plastic bags and pipes around them. As we arrive some of them make off. Freddy goes to talk to the handful who remain. They're young, he says – only teenagers. Even so, one apparently lifted his shirt to reveal a gun.

Many of these sites are run by gangs, who demand that locals work with them or suffer the consequences. People acquiesce, in part because they fear what will happen to them if they don't, and in part because there is precious little work around here and they need the money.

Word has it that the president and his cronies are benefiting from these illegal operations. Portraying his government as a friend

of nature, Maduro has created a Mining Arc, ostensibly to protect national parks, while, some claim, at the same time encouraging businessmen and locals to extract minerals where they can.

I can't wait to get away from this grim, degraded area. Arturo, my Pemon friend, has prepared lunch for us at his home village of Kamarata. So off we go, whirling above the rivers and the forest again. I could get used to a helicopter taxi service.

We land a few minutes later at a small settlement in a wide plain of open, cultivated land. There seems to be a policy in Venezuela to have the name of every town, village or city picked out in big, colourful, free-standing letters, sometimes several feet high. There's no question that this modest Pemon village is called Kamarata, as we have to walk around the name to reach the main street.

The Pemon people have lived in the area for centuries, but

they were nomadic until missionaries arrived and encouraged them to build permanent homes and settlements. The one building that stands out from all the others here is the church. It is tall, pedimented and painted entirely white, save for a single black cross above the entrance.

We walk up a red dirt track to Arturo's house, where he and his family have prepared lunch for us. It's hot and we gather round a table in the shade of a tin-roofed porch. A big mango tree stands nearby. Otherwise there's not much natural cover.

Arturo's wife and daughter have prepared a traditional meal for us. Laid out on a red-checked tablecloth is a fish stew with very hot peppers. On other dishes are cassava and plantain, and there is a bowl containing a particular type of worm that is found embedded in palm trees. The palm tree forms a vital part of people's lives here, providing

fruit, leaves for building roofs, fibre for making hammocks – as well as the nourishing delicacy that nestles in front of me.

If palm-tree worms aren't hard enough to contemplate eating, there's also a hot sauce made from manioc and ants' bottoms. I never really thought of ants as having bottoms but in Pemon country they do and these are much sought after.

I tuck in, knowing that I shall probably never again have a meal like this. It's strong-flavoured and tasty, and Joe, our sound man, tells me he catches a sharp crunching sound as I bite into an ant's bottom. Which is probably not something he'll record again for a while.

The family all eat together, reaching for the food unhurriedly. A light wind blows. Arturo, who speaks English, explains that the Pemon people were given generous land rights by Hugo Chávez, but that along with that came outside interference. Now, he says, his people like to keep

themselves to themselves. His face clouds over when I ask him about the gold prospecting. It's out of control, he thinks. He confirms what we saw for ourselves earlier by the river – that young people who have nothing else to do are being drawn in to work illegally by organised gangs.

Though I'm now in the mood for little more than an extended siesta, word comes back from our pilot that the cloud has lifted from the Angel Falls and that the most challenging leg of our Canaima trip can therefore now be attempted. We pile back into the helicopter and climb up and over the spectacular sweeping forest scenery, before rising up the precipitous walls of Auyán *tepui*, whose summit extends 270 square miles (700 square kilometres). It is from this massive platform – called Devil's Mountain – that the Angel Falls plunge over 2,600 feet (800 metres) to the ground.

The origin of the name is the one unextraordinary thing about this extraordinary natural phenomenon. The Angel Falls are named not after some mythical heavenly messenger, but after Jimmie Angel, an American pilot who flew over the area in 1933.

To the Pemon people it has always been Kerepakupai Merú (waterfall of the deepest place).

Quite suddenly the falls come into view. The setting is magnificent. Over the years the falling water has carved a funnel in the massive rock wall behind it, which acts like a frame around a painting, making the most of the lofty spill of water. This is the dry season, so the water tumbling off the top of the cliff is more impressive in height than power. It falls almost languidly, as if in slow motion. Where it hits the ground there is a small rocky platform which it strikes before careering on down into the valley below.

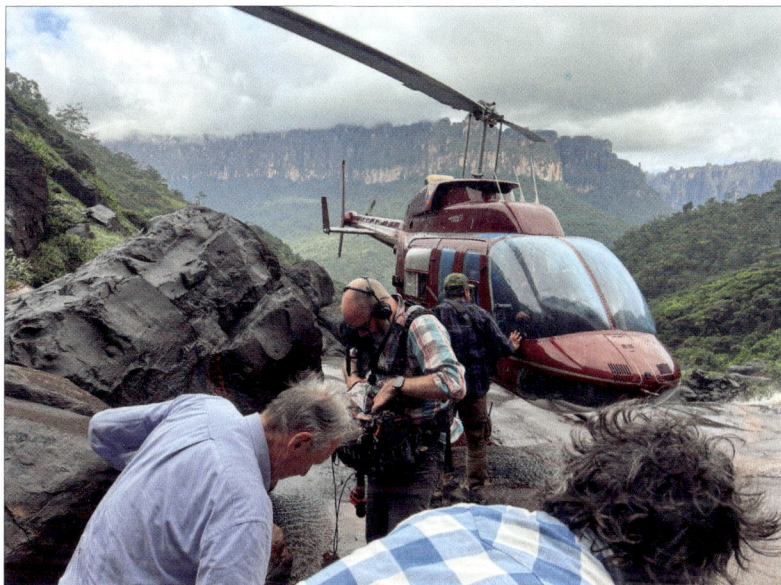

It is on this rocky platform, about half the length of a cricket pitch, that we are about to land. The sound of crashing water merges with the slowing thud of helicopter engines as we edge onto the tiniest slip of rock. All I can see outside is water streaming across the boulders onto which we are about to step. With exquisite care Freddy lowers us down. The helicopter's blades are a hair's breadth away from solid rock, but Freddy remains calm as he first lands the helicopter and then inches it forward until he can risk venturing no further.

Then it's all go. Our fixer pushes the door open and helps us out. We drop into running water on smooth stone. No one can afford to slip.

Heads down, we take cover, hanging on for dear life to two huge boulders. Our pilot reverses the chopper, turns and flies off the way we came. He will return in half an hour.

I don't think I've ever been confronted with nature quite as

dramatic as this. Above me falling water hits the ground just a few feet from where I'm standing. Behind me is the perilously slippery ledge on which we landed, hanging high above the great bowl of forest and rock below.

This is so completely and utterly magnificent a location that I barely notice that, for the second afternoon running, I'm completely sodden.

Then, of course, being human, my ecstasy is swiftly replaced by anxiety. Was it in twenty minutes or half an hour that our pilot said he would be returning? Will he be able to repeat the amazingly skilful manoeuvre that set us down here? How easy will it be to get back into the helicopter? What if I slip? I notice that Jaimie, plus camera, has already slithered to the ground, although he swiftly regains his footing and carries on filming.

Looking around I realise how – and indeed why – very few people have ever stood here. I wouldn't have missed this for the world. For me this is a necessary risk.

The sound of the helicopter breaks my reverie, and soon we are in and wheeling away. Tired, wet and insanely happy.

CANAIMA TO THE COAST

I SHALL MISS WAKU LODGE. I'M TEMPTED TO CALL IT WACKO
Lodge in view of the extraordinary adventures I've had here, and as
I walk to my last breakfast this morning it still has some surprises. A
tapir the size of a pig, with big eyes, a long snout and glowing, almost
wax-like skin, wanders into the bar. Two of the resident mongrel dogs
pursue it into the garden, where it's joined by a young tapir calf. The
dogs renew their half-hearted pursuit, but the tapirs trot away from
them, down to the lagoon and into the water where they splash about.
The dogs lose interest and wander off.

There's a toucan in residence in the dining room, and a monkey scampers about on the roof of reception as we check out. Thank you, Waku.

Out on the airstrip a small plane awaits to take us to a very different part of Venezuela. We fly north for three hours, re-crossing the mighty Orinoco, until we are over the coast and descending towards an atoll of sand-circled islands set among the strikingly clear waters of the Caribbean. Venezuela has a longer Caribbean coastline than any other country, and the islands we're going to sample are known collectively as Los Roques. We touch down on the only airstrip, on the mile-square island of Gran Roques. Cars are banned, so we walk across the soft, hot sand to our accommodation. The sun burns down, bouncing off the brilliant azure and turquoise waters on either side of us.

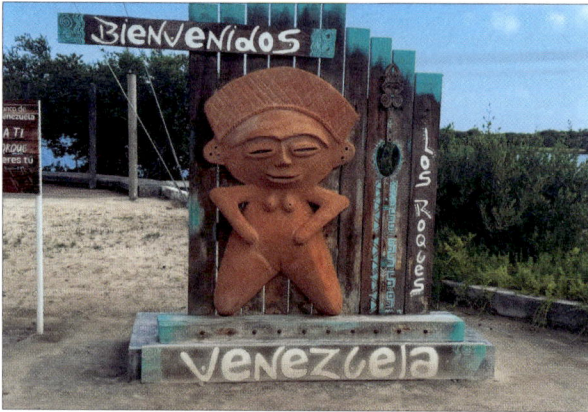

The old town is a homely, unpretentious gathering of wood-and-plaster houses, doing their best to protect themselves from the midday glare. Every now and then, though, there is evidence of money spent. Extravagant trophy houses are springing up wherever there's room. They're clearly as much for showing off as for living in. They bring a whiff of Californian ostentation to this otherwise simple fishing village.

There is still money to be made in Venezuela. But where once much of it would have been invested abroad, now the sanctions imposed by the US in 2017, in response to the political and economic turmoil of the Maduro presidency, are driving wealthy citizens to

spend it at home. With Caracas only a thirty-five-minute flight away the prospects for developers on Los Roques are looking very attractive. Hence the large houses on small islands.

As it turns out, our *posada*, called La Gaviota (The Seagull), is not one of these, but a small, beguiling house a few yards from the sea. Painted sky blue and white, it offers the merciful shade of a spreading grey mangrove tree out front, beneath which we eat a fine lunch of ceviche of barracuda. Out to sea a squadron of brown pelicans dive and scoop up fish into their shopping-bag beaks.

Our host is a bright-eyed, restlessly busy, kite-surfing Venezuelan called German Olavarría. His parents built La Gaviota as a second

home in the 1970s but, as they weren't using it a lot, he later persuaded them that it might be better employed as a *posada* – more of an inn than a hotel – which they, and he, would run.

German is keen to take us for a boat ride so that we can see more of the surrounding coral islands. These atolls, like Canaima, are part of a national park, one of forty-three in the country, hence, in part, their seductive, laid-back appeal. Certainly, the beach he takes us to across

the coral reefs is free from signs of development. Indeed, it's almost deserted. But as we make the return trip to Los Roques I spot quite a few recently built and expensive-looking seaside villas and exclusive hotels. This may be a national park, but, as German and his fellow small property owners fear, wealthy friends of the government seem to be able to get round any restrictions that might theoretically be in place.

In the evening I look out over the balcony outside my room and take in the sounds of the seafront: voices, music, and the slap of fishing boats at their moorings. And I can't help thinking, who wouldn't want a house here?

ROART - ALCALDE ALEXANDER CAMACHO EN HOMENA
ALDE ALEXANDER CAMACHO EN HOMENAJE AL COMA
R CAMACHO EN HOMENAJE AL COMANDANTE SUPREM
DE MIRANDA - ALCALDE ALEXANDER CAMACHO EN HOM

LOS ROQUES TO SANTA TERESA

NEVER MORE RELUCTANT TO LEAVE A HOTEL, WE BOARD a small propeller plane to Caracas. At the tiny airstrip at Los Roques an eagle-eyed security guard – well, in this case, security boy, looking no more than eighteen – searches my bags with laborious thoroughness and fierce concentration. With barely suppressed triumph, he lights on my bug spray, which I shall certainly need as we begin a long road journey into western Venezuela, and which no one else between London, Madrid and Caracas has spotted so far. In the bin it goes.

The flight from the Caribbean beaches to the domestic terminal at Caracas takes little more than half an hour. We then transfer to the convoy of vehicles which will take us south and west over the next few days. Freddy's team of drivers are specialists in adventurous travel and a cheery bunch. One of them, Lenny, speaks very good English, which is how I find out that he was named after Lenin.

Heading out of Caracas we have one last look at the sea from a fast-food lunch place at La Guaira, not far from the airport. As waves break on the rocks below, we sit on bar stools while red-uniformed staff, who look as young as my bug-spray confiscator, bring us *arepas* bulging with cheese or shrimp or pork and crushed avocado or whatever you want. Em remembers that when she was young a national tragedy took place right here. It was December 1999, and days of rain had created unstoppable mudslides from the cliffs above. They took the lives of some thirty thousand people. Despite the scale of the disaster she remembers Chávez being very reluctant to accept any outside help.

I look up at the high sandy slopes – now, despite their continuing vulnerability, re-occupied with what reminds me of a very

California-like resilience. A place for chancers and optimists. In fact, Venezuela keeps reminding me of the USA. The fast-food outlets like the one we're in now. The grid-pattern avenues of Caracas. The preponderance of Mack trucks on the highways, blasting past with their deep-throated bass roar.

It's scarcely surprising. In the oil-boom years that preceded Hugo Chávez's arrival on the scene, the two countries were joined at the hip, whatever the form of Venezuela's government at any given moment – democracy, civilian dictatorship or military dictatorship. Not any more. In 2019 Trump signed Executive Order 13884, freezing the assets of the Maduro government in the USA. Only a week before we arrived the new Trump administration announced that it would withdraw Temporary Protection Status from Venezuelans living in the US, using uncompromisingly harsh words.

'Remember,' said Kristi Noem, Trump's appointment to the Department of Homeland Security, 'Venezuela purposely emptied out their prisons, emptied out their mental health facilities and sent them to the United States of America.'

We take the road that tunnels its way, south and west, through an arm of the Andes. Our destination tonight is the Hacienda Santa Teresa, founded in 1796. It was bought by the Vollmer family in 1830 and has been producing Venezuela's finest rum since 1883.

After cramped hours in the Toyota our welcome at the hacienda is a magical surprise. We are shown into the old family house where there is much dark and gleaming wood furniture, a billiard table, shelves of old books and bottles of finest rum in glass display cases. A table is rather magnificently laid out for dinner, with cut glass and napkins,

and beyond it is a quiet courtyard garden with a stone well-head in the centre. Alberto Vollmer, who runs the family business, is a smart, articulate, energetic man, anxious to please. He is proud of the long history of Santa Teresa. He tells me the main building is two hundred years old. The patio was added about a century later.

Dinner is carrot soup, chicken pie and about the best chocolate mousse I've ever tasted. My room is just off the courtyard and it is palatial. It's quite a long walk from the door to the bed, especially after Alberto's generosity with the rum.

DAY
9

SANTA TERESA TO ACARIGUA

AS ALBERTO EXPLAINS TO US OVER A WONDERFULLY full breakfast, the old-fashioned charm, peace and quiet we are experiencing at the hacienda are rare commodities in the area. Though it might seem hard to believe as we pass the butter, the province we are in, Aragua, is one of the most violent in a violent country. Crime rocketed in the Chávez years, as social instability escalated and the economy began to disintegrate. Today, even the government has had to admit that Venezuela has one of the highest murder rates in the world. Over twenty-three thousand lives were taken in one year, 2018, alone. The country is now home to dozens of gangs that profit from prostitution, racketeering, drugs, illegal mining and kidnapping. One of the most notorious, the Tren de Aragua, has its roots in the district.

Over the years, various attempts have been made to tackle violent crime in Venezuela. Most have been ineffectual. And as the authorities have struggled, so gangs have spread their sphere of operations. Many now operate in the US as well as in South America. Formerly, those arrested in the US – who happened to include some of the most dangerous – were imprisoned there. Recently, however, the US has made it clear that it doesn't want them any more, and in the early months of 2025 alleged members of the Tren de Aragua were controversially dispatched to a maximum-security prison in El Salvador.

Alberto Vollmer acknowledges the crime problem, but he rejects conventional solutions. For him, the answer to Venezuela's epidemic of lawlessness lies less in punishment than in rehabilitation. For the past twenty years, therefore, he has sought to help convicted criminals find a new purpose in life via his favourite sport: rugby. The scheme he runs is called Project Alcatraz.

He speaks passionately about the successes he's had in using sport to bring about reconciliation and reintegration into society, and this morning he would like us to see Project Alcatraz at work.

We drive first to the nearby town of Revenga, which seems calm enough, with its multicoloured shops and a dazzlingly fresh-painted church. Back in 2017, however – when, in Alberto's view, the country reached its nadir – this was a lawless and dangerous place, in thrall to the Tren de Aragua. The gang's grip may have been broken, but Revenga, looking so comfortable in the morning sunshine, still has huge problems. There are children out on the streets who should be in school. There is no money to pay the teachers. And the community has lost some of its best people to emigration.

We follow Alberto through fields of sugar cane and along avenues of tall, waving palm trees to a very well-kept, full-size rugby field. Today both men's and women's teams will be playing. There's much waiting around. Then the bus with the male prisoners arrives. First out are the guards, rifles at the ready. They form a line around the door of the bus, and only when all the checks have been made are the first players allowed to step down. This ritual is repeated a few minutes later when the female prisoners arrive, already dressed in rugby gear.

Alberto swells with pride. He's keen to point out the success of the teams and certainly, when they get going, the standard is high. Their passing is swift, they move the ball well and they look as if they're enjoying themselves.

Alberto has a good relationship with the players. He particularly wants me to meet José, a thin-faced, intense young man, now

thirty-one, and out of prison after serving a sentence for murder. As a teenager he had been sent by his gang to slaughter an entire family, but after killing one member found himself unable to complete the assignment. He was arrested, jailed for many years, took drugs, reached the bottom. He talks in passionately grateful terms of what playing rugby in Project Alcatraz has meant to him, grateful for the chance he's been given to break the cycle of violence. 'Without it, I'd be dead by now,' he tells me.

Alberto has his photo taken with both the male and female teams. After that there is one final touching moment. Today's event, which occurs only once a year, not only gives the prisoners a brief respite from the rigours of incarceration, but also allows one or two family members to attend. The wife of one of the members of the men's team, who for practical reasons has been unable to see him for a while, is

given the opportunity to introduce him to their one-year-old baby. Joy unconfined. Then the armed guards gather around them and his father and the rest of his team are led back to the bus and back to prison.

As the boss of one of Venezuela's most successful businesses, Alberto Vollmer, one hopes, has some clout in the country. After seeing what he's achieved with the Alcatraz project it can only be a win for this beleaguered country if he can make rehabilitation government policy.

Before we leave the hacienda, we are given a tour of its impressive rum distillery. And then, in the afternoon we are back on the road and heading deeper into Los Llanos, the agricultural heartland of Venezuela, the land from which Hugo Chávez came, and the land of those to whom he was seeking to appeal when he brought in his

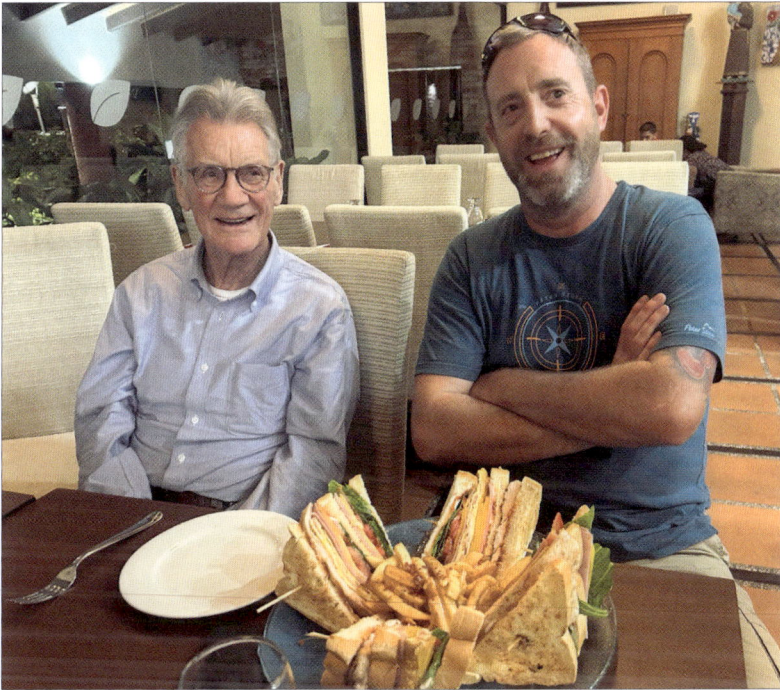

socialist policies. 'It is time the money reached the places where the majority live.' Not the wealthy Washington-pampered elite, but solid, hard-working, salt-of-the-earth farming folk. *El pueblo* – the people – he called them and to whom he felt himself to belong.

In the evening we reach Acarigua, to stay in a very efficient, well-appointed, business-orientated establishment. Nothing quaint, no period charm. In fact, I shall chiefly remember it for the size of its club sandwiches.

Archie, our medic, is brought one which looks like a small mountain range.

SABANETA TO HATO CRISTERO

IT'S A HOT AND CLAMMY MORNING AS WE SET OFF FOR Sabaneta, the town where Hugo Chávez was born. Though the roads are pretty good, some of the drivers on them certainly aren't and we're overtaken by fuel tankers driven at breakneck speeds. As we turn off the main highway we pass the charred shell of a tanker which careered off the road and exploded.

Sabaneta seems at first glance a sleepy place. An ordinary, low-rise town with no particular sense of distinction, or even pride, at being Chávez's birthplace.

But the further we drive into the centre the more we see Chávez's name on walls and posters, very often twinned with his hero Simón Bolívar.

AL HIJO ILUSTRE DEL
PUEBLO VENEZOLANO Y
COMANDANTE SUPREMO
HUGO RAFAEL CHÁVEZ FRÍAS
EN EL DIA DEL ANIVERSARIO
DE SU NATALICIO 28-07-2016 POR
ENCARGO DEL PRESIDENTE DE:
RUSIA VLADÍMIR PUTIN
EMPRESA PETROLERA ROSNEFT
PRESIDENTE IGOR SECHIN
ESCULTOR / S.KAZANTSEV

We pull up in the Plaza del Estudiante, at the centre of which is an ugly mess of a statue. Chávez stands, punching the air, atop a mound of inexplicable grey imagery. Such a contrast with the jaunty rearing horses of the Bolívar memorials elsewhere in the country.

A plaque beneath shows it to be a gift from Vladimir Putin.

We try to make the most of whatever shade we can find beneath the sparse covering of trees while we wait for our interviewees. One of them, an author who has a library of old books on Chávez, has already arrived. Before we can start filming him, a National Guardsman in caramel-coloured fatigues appears and starts to ask questions about our intentions here.

Freddy shows him the various authorisations we have, but then a car draws up and the guardsman is joined by a man and a woman in civilian clothes. They ask more questions and demand to see our passports.

We sit and wait while endless discussions go on. Phones are produced and information shared in long conversations with someone

somewhere. On a vivid mural across the road a young-looking Chávez gazes back at us.

By now more people have arrived to join the discussion. I think they are local police. No one seems to have the authority to make any decisions, but Freddy indicates to us that things are looking hopeful.

No sooner has he said this than it gets a whole lot more serious. A half-dozen very unsmiling men in black pile out of a van and come towards us. They are wearing helmets and body armour and carry M16 rifles.

On their backs is the acronym SEBIN, for Servicio Bolivariano de Inteligencia Nacional. The Intelligence Service.

The whole atmosphere changes now. Fewer smiles, no more side conversations, and certainly no prospect of filming.

At a sign from the men from SEBIN we get into our vehicles and follow them to the grounds of a local school, which seems to be empty. No teachers, as in Revenga?

The military intelligence people ask us to unload and open up our luggage. Everything, from mikes and camera batteries to unwashed socks and underpants, is duly noted and photographed.

The day drags on into the afternoon. We tell our guards that none of us has eaten since very early this morning, and they agree that we can have some lunch provided we are escorted. We follow them to the Camoruco, an inconspicuous nearby restaurant with football playing loudly on the TV screens.

We have a round of Polar beers, while the men from SEBIN, encumbered with their rifles and body armour, try their best to look vigilant and relaxed at the same time.

The mood changes perceptibly when one of our escorts manages to google my name on his phone, and soon they are gathered round, looking in some puzzlement at a forty-five-year-old YouTube clip of John Cleese and myself defending *The Life of Brian* in a heated argument with Malcom Muggeridge and the Bishop of Southwark. Soon they've found Monty Python and as they watch the Fish Slapping Dance I sort of know that, whatever else happens, we shan't be spending a night in jail.

We now learn why we have aroused such suspicion. Apparently, in protest at the Maduro government's re-election, there has been a spate of attacks on Chávez statues around the country, and the authorities have, accordingly, become jumpy. When a local official noted our presence in Sabaneta this morning he immediately contacted his superiors.

They in turn passed the message up the chain of command until it reached Military Intelligence HQ in Caracas. Fortunately, Freddy has managed to call a few contacts of his own back in the capital. After hours of waiting around, we are finally informed that we are free to go.

By now I've become something of a local celebrity. The men with guns request a group photo with me and I am invited to go and meet the Mayor of Sabaneta, a burly, youngish man who welcomes me to his town and promises to do all he can to help us.

Unfortunately he can't turn the clock back, so filming that was due to begin at 10.00 in the morning now can't get under way until 6.00 in the evening. We have just enough light to complete an interview with a sprightly white-haired local who was a childhood friend of Chávez. He remembers him warmly, could see his leadership ambitions from very early on, but sadly their friendship didn't survive Chávez's growing fame.

With filming for the day finally completed, it proves quite disorientating to arrive so late at our place for the night. It's way out in the countryside – a working ranch farm called Hato Cristero. My room, which I need torchlight to find, is in a dark corner of the property and has three beds, a hammock, and a door that barely opens. I set to unpacking my bags once again.

Over a hearty farm dinner we talk over the difficult day we've had and agree what a pity it was that we couldn't film most of it. Our experience has confirmed our inkling that we are seen as suspicious, and that that's the likely fate of any visitor to this stunning country. Fingers crossed for the days ahead.

Decide to sleep in bed number one.

DAY 11

HATO CRISTERO TO MÉRIDA

I AM WOKEN EARLY THIS MORNING, BUT VERY HAPPILY lie there listening to the rich avian choir outside my cabin. It's as if the BBC Natural History Unit are playing their entire library of recordings at the same time.

This is very much cowboy – or, rather, *llanero* – country. The dark wood dining room where we gather for breakfast is decorated with saddles, reins and bridles, and Armando, a tall, strapping *llanero* who works for the family who own this large *hato*, proudly tells us about the amount of wheat they grow and the number of cattle they rear.

In recent years, the cattle business has struggled in much the same way as other sectors of the economy, so it's perhaps not surprising that, according to Armando, his family make more money these days from showing tourists the wildlife than they do from their labour on the

farm. As though to demonstrate the point, he announces that he has an anaconda he wants to show me. Apparently he found it on a nearby road and this morning will be returning it to the wild. It is, he informs us, over 12 feet long (3.6 metres) and weighs 30 pounds (14 kilos).

When I ask him where it is, he grins and jabs his thumb towards his bulging rucksack. My jaw drops. I can't really believe that my first-ever encounter with an anaconda is to help extricate it from someone's backpack, but this is what I find myself doing, with expert help, in a wet and very muddy field after breakfast.

As this splendid creature uncoils itself, slowly and apparently endlessly, it reveals a handsome pattern of black rings with yellow circles on an olive-green background. One of the rangers is keen to point out its genital area down at the far end, which is a beautiful shade of deep gold. Sniffing the air, the snake seems to grow and thicken.

Anacondas, like pythons, are constrictors and squeeze their prey to death. The combination of its thickness and the rippling of its newly released muscles is an impressive display of awesome power. It's a struggle for four of us to hang on to it before it slithers away and disappears into a sea of mud.

We have quite an audience. White ibis and egrets stalk elegantly about. The surrounding trees are full of noisy squawking emanating from large, rather ungainly birds the size of small turkeys. Freddy told me that these are a very distinctive tropical bird called the hoatzin which nest in trees overlooking water. They have small heads topped with a strikingly punk crest, and blue faces. What makes them truly special is that their young are born with two bone spurs on each wing. These act as hooks, so that if any predator comes along, the chicks can drop into the water below and clamber out later using the hooks. An evolutionary byway which doesn't seem to have led anywhere else.

If we had more time I'd spend it learning about the birds of Los Llanos, 323 species of which flourish around here. Trogon and tanager, harpy eagles, roadside hawks, falcons and osprey. Perhaps I might even have caught a glimpse of the troupial, Venezuela's national bird. So much to see, if you know what you're looking for.

After the excitement of our encounter with an anaconda, our quest for other creatures that share this wetland area proves less successful. A herd of capybara, the world's largest rodent, seem to know what we're up to and take off at our approach. We then spend a long time trying to lure two spectacled caimans, a particularly evil-looking kind of alligator, out of the water. The first things we glimpse of the caiman – and the things from which this species draws its name – are two black-ringed eyes that pop up above the water like mini-periscopes. Armando and the other rangers dangle raw meat from the ends of long sticks in an intriguing game of cat and mouse. Curious to see what's on the ends of the sticks the eyes move slowly and cautiously closer to the bait.

Then they appear to lose interest and vanish beneath the surface. Fresh meat is produced and dangled out. Armando repeatedly strikes the surface with his stick to mimic juicy prey in the water. After quite a long time the eyes re-emerge, followed by a raising of bodies. It's quite a shock to see for the first time just how big caiman are and how menacing their quivering spines appear. We hold our breath. Closer and closer they come. Their jaws part in readiness. But only inches away from the meat, something spooks them, they snap into a violent somersault and, with a last thrash of the tail, disappear below the water.

I realise now why wildlife cameramen have to hide in bushes for

days just to get a single shot. Nature can't be hurried. Unfortunately, we can't afford days in bushes.

As it happens, there is a fall-back photo opportunity in the shape of Romulo, an enormous Orinoco caiman who has been domesticated and will happily emerge from a protectively fenced pond in the grounds of the *hato* and frighten the life out of guests with a deep growl and snap of jagged-toothed jaws.

After these few days in the hot, sticky flatlands of Los Llanos we turn west into a cool valley that runs between increasingly high mountains. These are the Andes – the backbone of South America that passes through seven countries and runs for 5,000 miles from the shores of the Caribbean south to Patagonia. We're now on the Trans-Andean highway. 'It's a beautiful road,' Freddy told us before we left; but it's also narrow and places to stop are accordingly hard to find. 'Use the loo now.'

When this highway was built way back in the 1920s and '30s to connect the Andean region with the rest of Venezuela it was considered a marvel of engineering. Much of it was constructed by political prisoners.

It winds tortuously up through steep-sided valleys, which occasionally broaden out to allow space for agriculture and room for small market towns to grow and spread on the terraces above the rivers. This was once the home of the Timoto-Cuica, indigenous agriculturists who were building and cultivating these terraces long before Europeans came to South America.

We continue climbing above the treeline onto the dry, sparsely populated Andean plateau, or *páramo*, home to cactus and giant rosette plants. We are now thousands of feet above the plains of Los Llanos. This is the land of the Andean condor, the largest flying bird in the world. All we need to do is keep going, but, alarmingly, one of our vehicles is overheating and has to pull over. Ironic that we should coast through the steam and humidity of the plains, only to boil over at the coolest point of our journey so far. Freddy estimates that we are up at 3,500 metres. I make that over 11,000 feet.

Occasional trucks emerge from the low cloud and grind past as our drivers gather round the steaming radiator offering solutions. In the end the problem is solved, or quite possibly postponed, and we continue up to the highest point of the mountain chain, or *cordillera*, some 13,000 feet above sea level. There's light snow swirling around us, and the cloud comes and goes, alternating total white-outs with snatched glimpses of magnificently vivid alpine views.

Finally, we're over the top and down along the winding road that takes us to the outskirts of Mérida.

We pull into the entrance of the Estancia La Cañada, a *posada* built into the mountainside. The location is stunning, but all we want after our epic journey over the mountains is several beers and a good meal. The *estancia* – or estate – has both, as well as something we thought extinct outside Caracas – a wine list.

★ DAY ★
12

MÉRIDA

DESPITE AN ALL-CONSUMING TIREDNESS I FOUND IT difficult to get to sleep last night. Whenever I nodded off I was jerked sharply back to consciousness to find myself panting quite heavily, my breath coming in short gasps.

At first I blamed the wine list. But I had no headache. I lay as still as I could and waited for my system to calm down. But it didn't. Five years ago I had open-heart surgery with one valve replaced and another repaired. The physical pressures of our journey so far, moving rapidly through so many different conditions, must have put my patched-up ticker under extreme stress. What was I thinking, clambering about behind waterfalls, holding anacondas? Were these hard-won breaths payback for years of pretending I was still twenty-seven? Didn't the great DJ John Peel have a fatal heart attack in the Andes?

My imagination, compounded by my inability to sleep, now raced forward to the end of my life. What would Channel 5 do with a journey halfway round Venezuela? Had I told my children where all my passwords are kept? Would they play 'Always Look on the Bright Side' at my funeral?

And then, amid my racing thoughts, I remembered that I had been through this before, while filming the Annapurna Trail in the Himalayas.

The same sleepless nights, the same thumping heartbeat as my lungs strained to find the oxygen that was suddenly in short supply.

Despite the fact that I'd been in the Andes for only half a day, I was, I finally realised, suffering from common-or-garden altitude

sickness. The rate of ascent from ground level to 13,000 feet in a matter of hours had produced the same response from my system as three days spent at high altitude in Nepal.

I looked at my bedside clock. It was half-past two and all was silent.

The awareness of knowing that I'd been through this before, albeit when I was twenty-one years younger, calmed me; and though Archie, our medic, was just a phone call away, I decided not to show any vulnerability by ringing for help. Very British.

This morning it turns out that the only other member of our team to have suffered such severe symptoms is Archie. He has just enough energy to give me a full check-up on the balcony.

What really makes me feel better is where we are. When we arrived last night it was getting dark, so nothing has prepared me for the magnificence of the surroundings.

Sunlight is creeping across the mountain ranges which rise high above the slopes and terraces of the well-kept gardens of our *estancia*. We do some gentle filming and I sit for a while beneath a spreading avocado tree and take it all in. It is good to be alive, and despite the scares I could very happily stay here another night. We all could.

Mérida – or to give it its full name, Santiago de los Caballeros de Mérida – is one of the main cities of the Venezuelan Andes. Founded by the Spanish in the sixteenth century it remained relatively inconspicuous until access roads were built in the 1920s. Now it's a university city with seventeen thousand students. It's a flourishing destination for adventure sports, and home to the Heladería Coromoto, an ice-cream parlour recognised by Guinness World Records as offering more flavours than any other. More free thinking, less corporate than Caracas, the city has seen many of the largest anti-Maduro protests. It's an attractive, colourful, unflashy place, enhanced by the clarity and brightness of the mountain air around it.

There's another world record held by Mérida. It is the home of the Teleférico Mukumbari, the highest cable-car ride in the world. It runs from the centre of Mérida to Pico Espejo, the summit of the Cordillera de Mérida, 15,629 feet (4,765 metres) above sea level.

Just the thing for someone recovering from altitude sickness.

Despite feeling a little wobbly after last night, I can't pass up a chance to try the highest cable-car trip in the world. What would I tell my grandchildren if I turned down such an opportunity?

The *teleférico* opened in the 1960s, then was closed, but reopened after a major facelift in 2016. It's reassuringly clean and efficient.

The gondolas are big, with room for forty people in each one. There are four separate stages to the ride, with terminals at each one, so you don't have to go to the very top.

Thankfully I feel fine, with only the slightest sense of light-headedness every now and then, and the panoramic view of Mérida below is worth the ticket price alone. At each stage the surroundings become wilder. Mérida vanishes from view as we're hauled up through forest and into the clouds. After an hour we're near the summit. The trees have gone and we're enclosed by sheer rock walls. Once again I have a sense of the drama of the Venezuelan landscape. I'm also in awe of the extraordinary feat of engineering that has brought me up here.

The ascent is not without risks: all the way to the top there are graphic warnings of the symptoms of pulmonary oedema. *'Accelerated respiration'* (which I know only too well), *'Sensation of nausea'*, *'Tightness of the thorax'*. It's not entirely surprising. After all, people are being taken to over half the height of Everest in less than an hour.

At the summit, there's a huge national flag, billowing out majestically in the wind. Venezuelans love their flag and I know it well now. The three bright horizontal colours: gold, representing the wealth of the country; blue, the ocean that separates it from Spain; and red, the blood spilt during the independence wars. The eight stars in the centre represent the seven provinces that signed the Declaration of Independence in 1811, and Guyana, which joined in 1817.

I join the mostly young crowd walking around, taking in the view. Many of them are wearing skimpy outfits that seem more suited to a nightclub than a mountain top. Smartphones are in everyone's hands.

I take a photo of the peak of Mount Humboldt. Until recently it was the home of Venezuela's last and largest glacier. But global warming over the past twenty years initially caused it to shrink and then to disappear altogether, making Venezuela the first country in the

Andes to lose all her glaciers. It's become a cause célèbre for environmental activists here in Mérida. I notice that their information boards sit alongside the health warnings in the various cable-car stations.

In the afternoon I explore the heart of the city with Diana, a twenty-three-year-old student at the University of the Andes. Even though the city is not well-disposed to Maduro or his folksy TV image, the need to be careful about what you say holds as much here as it does elsewhere in the country, and as we stroll around the obligatory tree-shaded Bolívar Square, I get the sense that Diana is choosing her words very carefully. There's clearly something of a disconnect between what she wants to say and what she's prepared to be seen saying.

The atmosphere has become more tense since the disputed 2024 election, she tells me. Political activists who oppose Maduro have ended up in jail. Security has been tightened. Diana herself can no longer use social media as freely as before.

At her house I meet two friends of hers. One of them, a twenty-eight-year-old film-maker, is less guarded than Diana. She is happy to be known as a political activist, she says. Indeed, she's currently making her views known through a film project that tells the contrasting stories of a Venezuelan who chooses to leave the country, as so many millions have done, and one who chooses to stay behind.

Diana's other friend works as a nutritionist. She is quietly and desperately frustrated. 'People are going hungry,' she says. There is no money for her work, and many of the doctors have left.

These bright and critical young women should be the future of Venezuela. They have chosen to stay and make their country more open, more welcoming, more benevolent. But such is the government's grip that they have to stay in the shadows, while Super Moustache and the press he controls take the spotlight.

By way of an example, the three women show me on their phones the 'V app' which people are encouraged to use to report any anti-government activities.

The Posada del Sol, where we will be staying for the next two nights, is a compact and attractive little hotel tucked away in a network of narrow streets in downtown Mérida. It's been run since it opened twenty years ago by a formidable German lady. There is a small patio garden at the back and, at reception, the finest selection of books about Venezuela I've seen since we arrived in the country. This is a most beneficial coincidence, for tomorrow is our first and only day off. After twelve days of continuous travelling and filming we can have a breather, get laundry done and, in my case, make the best of the German lady's travel library.

★ DAY ★
14

MÉRIDA TO LAKE MARACAIBO

RESTED AND REVIVED, WE SET OUT TO COMPLETE OUR girdling of the country, though there's much to do before we see Caracas again. Already there are complications. Of a really quite unexpected kind.

The plan was to overnight in hammocks in the small fishing village of Ologa on the shores of Lake Maracaibo, from where we would hopefully see the Catatumbo lightning, a Guinness World Records phenomenon. Scientists estimate that lightning makes a record 1.6 million strikes in the skies above the lake every year, with up to forty flashes a minute on a stormy night. It occurs on 140–160 days of the year, so there's more than a chance we could be lucky.

However, word has come through that Ologa has been hit by something less spectacular but no less dramatic: an invasion of yellow-tail moths. At breeding season, they emerge from the surrounding jungle in huge numbers, attracted to any light source. Hairs from the females fill the air. If caught on the skin, or ingested through the mouth, they can cause extreme discomfort.

There's much jocular talk of Revenge of the Killer Moths, but no one wants to disbelieve what hardened locals take so seriously. Communications with the lakeside village are primitive, and we won't know how things are for sure until we get there. It'll be a long journey, requiring a drive to the lake and a three-hour boat journey on to Ologa. We reckon, though, that it's worth the risk.

Any road in the Andes is by definition spectacular, and as we weave our way out of the mountains, we find ourselves in a corridor between high, wide slopes of sandy, sedimentary rock carved out by the river. Dazzling purple and magenta bougainvillea catch the morning sun.

Via a series of tunnels we emerge from the mountains and into increasingly rich rainforest.

We join the queue at a *peaje*, a tollbooth, which you find at the borders of all twenty-three of Venezuela's states. We are now crossing from Mérida into Zulia state, which, with its capital Maracaibo, is the most populous of them all.

The rainforest gives way to rich savannah land. Here palm-oil and banana plantations are interspersed with spreading acacia trees, mangoes and tall, red-trunked ceibas with their distinctively fan-shaped roots.

A long, dead-straight stretch of country road brings us to the small town of Puerto Concha, where we unload all our luggage from the vehicles and transfer it to two unromantic plastic-hulled fishing boats. We've heard nothing further about possible moth attacks, so, hoping for the best, we decide to carry on to Ologa.

The 5,000-square-mile (13,000 square-kilometre) expanse of Lake Maracaibo is in effect the biggest inland body of water in South America, though, as it has a narrow northern inlet from the Caribbean, it's not technically a lake. We access it via the delightful estuary of the Concha river. The river here is just the right size, neither too wide nor too straight. White herons rise languidly from purple-flowered beds of water hyacinth, and wheel and swoop from one bank to the other.

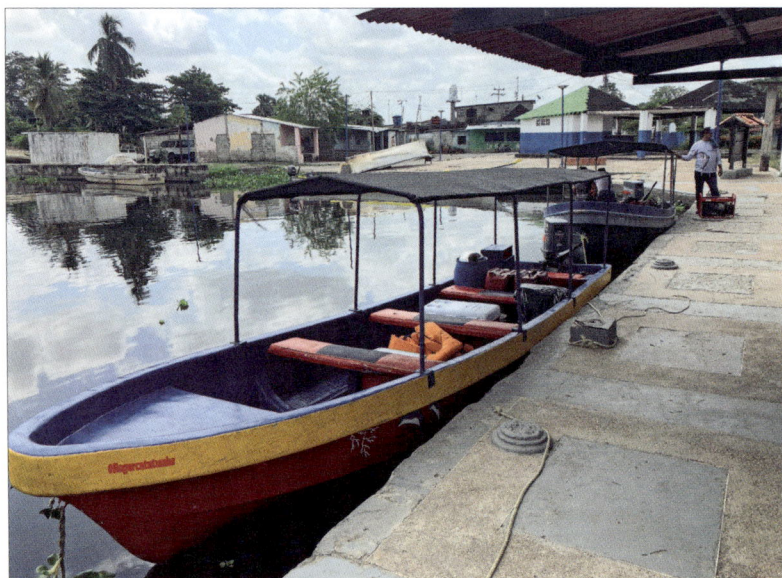

Nature at her most soothing. I have to pinch myself to remind me that I am where I am.

Then everything changes abruptly. The river meets the lake and we're suddenly exposed. No green, bird-filled banks or picturesque bends. Instead there are waves and dark waters stretching away to the horizon. The ride becomes less pleasurable, more functional as the boatmen accelerate and we whack and smack our way across the choppy surface.

On the way to Ologa we come across some fishermen who are out on the water looking for the much-sought-after blue crab. Their catch may be valuable, but their technique is very basic. With two men to each boat, they first set out lines of chicken heads as bait. Then one of the men sits cross-legged in the bow and, as his companion drives the boat along the line, he scoops up the feasting crabs in a square-boxed

net at the end of a long pole, flicking the contents into a bucket on the deck. It must be back-breaking work, but it's done deftly and skilfully. Maracaibo blue crab will fetch near to $40 a kilo on the open market. The fishermen who gather them are paid 96 cents a kilo.

Eventually we catch sight of our destination. Ologa materialises as a collection of low shacks built out onto the lake on stilts. They call these stilted constructions *palafitos*, loosely translated on Google as 'overwater bungalows'.

We gratefully disembark and meet our prospective host. He confirms what we had hoped not to hear: that we would be taking a dangerous risk if we were to sling our hammocks here tonight.

The moths arrived in such numbers last night, he tells us, that he and his family had to close every door, board up all the windows, switch

off any light that might attract them, and sit and wait for the swarm to move on. (Though I didn't know it at the time, I now know that the collective noun for moths is an eclipse.)

Moths are very far from being the only problem Ologa faces. Although it's a lovely spot, it's also an economically distressed one. The fishermen earn barely enough to scrape a living. The local school has closed, leaving the children to play around listlessly, kicking a football or chasing the dogs, which in turn chase the pigs. No government help is on hand. A sense of resignation hangs in the air.

The village huts, which are of the simplest design, don't look robust enough to withstand a major moth eclipse, let alone a conventional tempest. A nearby village on stilts, they tell us, recently collapsed altogether for lack of attention. The irony is that the country owes its

name to such houses. The first Europeans who came here, finding that most communities lived on the water, were reminded of a city nearer home. So they called the country Little Venice – Venezuela.

Sadly, just as the evening light is making this place look entrancing, we are left with no choice but to set out on another long boat ride back to the mouth of the Concha river, where there is a *palafito* on which we can stay overnight and watch the lightning display.

The mood is subdued. No one likes to feel they've been defeated by a bunch of moths.

The sun has set by the time we reach our home for the night. Less an overwater bungalow than a pillbox raised on stubby concrete legs, it makes the *palafitos* of Ologa look like palaces. To rub salt in the wound, we spot, just across the water, a much more manicured platform with lights and a bar and proper accommodation. It turns out to be for guests of one of the smartest hotels in Maracaibo.

But in the end, I'm sure we have a lot more fun than they do. While Freddy and his team hang our hammocks by the light powered from a single rheumatic generator, a group of ladies from Puerta Concha put together some supper. And it is sensational. On this concrete platform in the middle of a lake they have prepared what is one of the best meals of the journey. Blue crab, boiled or grilled, delicious and abundant. Local beef, accompanied by chicken and chorizo, is beautifully tender. And all served with a fine salad and various crispy breads, washed down with the local Zulia beer, which is generally agreed to be the tastiest so far. For those with real stamina, a bottle of the finest Santa Teresa rum is opened as a digestif, bringing back memories of rugby players and men with guns.

To spare the generator the lights are turned off before the end of the meal, leaving people to find – and sometimes struggle to get into – their hammocks by the glow of their smartphone torches. Two of the hammocks have not been properly secured and drop their occupants on the floor in the early hours of the night. Silence falls briefly until one heavy snorer begins to recreate, and maintain, the sound of waves breaking on the shore.

Sadly, the Catatumbo lightning never makes an appearance. My dream of us all wrapped in blankets, drinking rum and gasping in awe and wonder at nature's spectacular light show, remains precisely that – a dream. Unlike the world's tallest waterfall or the world's highest cable car, this is one Venezuelan superlative I shan't be able to tell my grandchildren about.

Though I'm not so sure. On my way back from the loo at two o'clock, I swear I saw flashes of light on the far side of the lake. Either that or I hit my head on a beam. Anyway, next morning, our director is happy to record this as a sighting.

✦ DAY ✦
15

TO MARACAIBO

AFTER BREAKFAST WE LEAVE THE SLEEPY TOWN OF Puerto Concha and the men and women who looked after us so well the night before.

After yesterday's experience at Ologa it's hard not to associate Lake Maracaibo with people living on the edge of poverty, and yet beneath its dark surface lie the hydrocarbon-rich deposits which at one time made Venezuela the wealthiest country in South America. Over the next two days we'll see more of what and why the country did what it did with this bounty.

An hour or so later we've turned onto what Freddy tells us is the Pan-American Highway.

There's certainly a resonance to being on a road that runs 19,000 miles (30,000 kilometres) from Alaska to Argentina. I fall to imagining some of the great addresses it would make possible. 12483 Pan-American Highway or, better still, 12483b Pan-American Highway. Or even 180000 Pan-American Highway (*'Please leave at 179999 if out'*).

Alas, the reality is not as glamorous as the name. The highway, which officially opened in 1960, is a ragbag of interconnecting roads, and this bumpy section of two-lane road up from the city of El Vigía is a far cry from the swirling *autopistas* around Caracas. There's something embattled about the places we pass. At a filling station the girl who takes the money sits behind what looks like a cell door, and payment has to be pushed in between the bars.

The roadblocks are more numerous than elsewhere, and passports are more regularly checked.

We're travelling through a monotonous agricultural landscape. Cattle sheltering from the heat. Fruit plantations. The small towns we pass look increasingly downtrodden. Litter blows everywhere – something you'd never see in Caracas or Mérida. There is a pervading sense that all is not well here and I'm told that the UK Foreign Office has issued a red warning against travel in the area.

Freddy explains the instability. Colombia, whose border lies not far away, is caught up in a long-running civil war, and many Colombians are seeking refuge in Venezuela. Tensions are accordingly running high. It doesn't help that we happen to be travelling through the region at carnival time. The roads are busier than usual. Security is being tightened up.

It's hot now. Up to 32° Celsius, and for the first time since we arrived in Venezuela it starts to rain. Which I'm assured it shouldn't be doing as this is February and it's still the dry season.

It's at this point that we spot, by the side of the road and seemingly appearing from nowhere, a number of nodding donkeys, or pumpjacks as they used to be called. They look quaint, as if preserved to show how oil was extracted in the early days. But more and more come in sight and I realise they must still be productive. A little further on, thick pipelines, sometimes half-buried, run along the verge of the road. The grass around them has been burnt back.

Above us, pylons over 65 feet (20 metres) high carry power lines across the road and into the distance. We are in oil country and it's not romantic.

Oil was first discovered on this eastern shore of Lake Maracaibo in 1914, but the sheer scale of the deposits was not revealed until eight years later when an oil well, Barroso II, exploded near the village of Cabimas, pumping out 100,000 barrels of crude oil every day for almost a month. Within twenty years Venezuela was the third-biggest oil producer on the globe (indeed, it still has 304 billion barrels of crude oil reserves, some 18 per cent of the world's total). There was much money to be made here, so it is scarcely surprising that, with the help of US technology and investment, oil from Lake Maracaibo proceeded to finance a vibrant Venezuelan economy. Hotels on tops of mountains, elaborate and expensive road networks, world-leading cable-car systems – all made possible by oil profits.

Oil may have made the country wealthy, but that wealth was not equally shared among its citizens. When Hugo Chávez won the presidency on a socialist agenda in 1998, he accordingly redirected much of the profit that oil generated to redress the imbalance between the nation's relatively few rich and its numerous poor. A few years later he went a step further. Though the oil industry had been nationalised as the PDVSA back in 1976 (it's still colloquially referred to as Pedevesa) it was largely staffed by US and European companies. In 2003 Chávez fired nineteen thousand PDVSA employees and gave their jobs to his Venezuelan supporters. This grand gesture ignored the fact that the newcomers had little expertise or training to take over such a huge and complex business. Years of low investment and poor maintenance followed, causing production to fall. A decline in global oil prices at the end of the decade added to the country's woes. All too soon, Venezuela's golden days were over.

Despite periodic spikes in the income from oil since, those golden days have never returned. In 1974, according to one estimate, oil revenues were worth $4,582 to each Venezuelan citizen. By 2019 that figure was down to $572.

What with all the roadside checks, it has taken us the best part

of seven hours to drive to Maracaibo, Venezuela's second-biggest city. But at last, as the sun is setting, we find ourselves on the last stretch of the journey, a straight six-lane road called the Lara Zulia Highway. It must have been built in the heyday of the oil industry. Today it's almost deserted.

A much grander monument to the boom days looms ahead of us in the dusty twilight. Six massive 300-foot (90-metre) columns carry the road over the lake and into the city. Completed in 1962, this bridge, named after General Rafael Urdaneta, a contemporary of Bolívar's,

is five and a half miles long. If this were a movie the music would be soaring as we rise across the water and down into Maracaibo.

But there the grandeur ends and reality intrudes. Turning off the bridge we drive through streets of run-down housing, locked, barred and often abandoned buildings, pathways dimly lit and litter-strewn. Presumably in its days of glory, this area supplied goods and labour for a thriving oil industry. Now it looks like a ghost town. Darkness falls, adding a sense of threat. But gradually the living, working city materialises. We follow the grid-pattern roads towards the centre where the lights are brighter; and finally, beside a huge, seemingly empty residential block, we arrive at the doors of the Inter Maracaibo hotel, and our long day's journey comes to an end. No hammocks tonight. And no generators. And no blue crab for dinner.

★ DAY ★
16

MARACAIBO

NICE THOUGH THE INTER MARACAIBO IS, WE HAD hoped to stay at the Hotel Del Lago, a symbol of the oil-boom days, where American execs once rolled up in pink Cadillacs. It's still in business, but it's owned by the Venezuelan government, and lawyers have advised us that if we stay there we will be breaking US sanctions.

As it is, we've already lost our first interviewee of the day – a television journalist known to be critical of the current regime. Freddy and his team of drivers have asked that we don't interview him, as they would be associating themselves, and their business, with a high-profile critic of the government. Of course, we respect this. We know by now that the government can come down hard on critics and those who give them a platform to speak. We'll be long gone when our series goes public, but Freddy and the drivers will still be here and the regime will surely have kept an eye on them. When it comes to spying on its

citizens Maracaibo has a reputation comparable to that of Caracas. The thought that people may well be watching us from parked cars makes us all a bit jumpy.

We venture out on the streets. Once again I sense the parallels with cities in the United States, except in this case Detroit comes to mind rather than Los Angeles. Few people on the sidewalks. Cars speeding by. Businesses and shops with locked doors and screens over the windows. The good times seem to have passed.

I meet up with a young architect who is happy to speak to us. He's a corrective to our gloom. He likes it here – finds that there is work to do and that the city is good for someone like himself starting out. He won't hear a word against Chávez, whose mass sackings of skilled oil employees he blames on sanctions imposed on the government because it was socialist.

He himself seems to have worked out a neat way to avoid US sanctions. His office is not dependent on the government. He and his colleagues are freelance. They work online to produce schemes and designs for any customer anywhere in the world. Ironically, his work at the moment is with companies in the USA.

As the hot day advances I find myself becoming increasingly enamoured of Maracaibo. It may be wounded but it's certainly not dead. It has a big-city presence. An unapologetic sense of independence. Its lakeside walk is part of yet another of Venezuela's national parks and a well-kept place to wander, though it's probably best not to ask about the levels of pollution in the water it overlooks.

Eventually, I find myself at a small, congenial establishment called the Pa' Que Luis. It's a folksy place on the corner of downtown streets of well-preserved, colourfully painted period houses. Inside,

it consists of a bar leading to a long narrow room with photos and newspaper clippings pasted on the walls. It doesn't look as if it's changed in fifty years. And that's what makes it so attractive. This is not crumbling corporate Maracaibo. This is how it was before the oil boom.

It's here that I'm to meet Miss Zulia, winner of one of the twenty-three regional heats of the Beauty Queen of Venezuela competition, and only narrowly pipped at the post for the crown itself. The beauty contest, it has to be said, is something of a Venezuelan obsession, and it's an arena in which Venezuelan women have proved particularly successful. In fact, they have won more international titles than the women of any other country, having notched up seven Miss Universes, six Miss Worlds, nine Miss Internationals and two Miss Earths. (Though none appears to have won the coveted title which I once saw in a UK building magazine – Miss Construction.)

What makes Miss Zulia's success particularly significant is that she comes from the 400,000-strong Wayuu people, who live in northern Colombia and north-west Venezuela. They were here before the Spanish, and resisted attempts by the Catholic Church to assimilate them. Today they are famous for the beautifully abstract, vividly coloured textiles they weave. Miss Zulia is something of a neighbourhood hero, not just for her beauty but for her determined activism in fighting for the rights of Venezuela's indigenous people.

There's a buzz of excitement as word goes round that she's about to arrive, as if royalty were on its way. And she is a regal figure: tall and poised, with a strikingly beautiful oval face, long black hair piled in a bun, and intense dark eyes. She wears a floor-length sky-blue robe

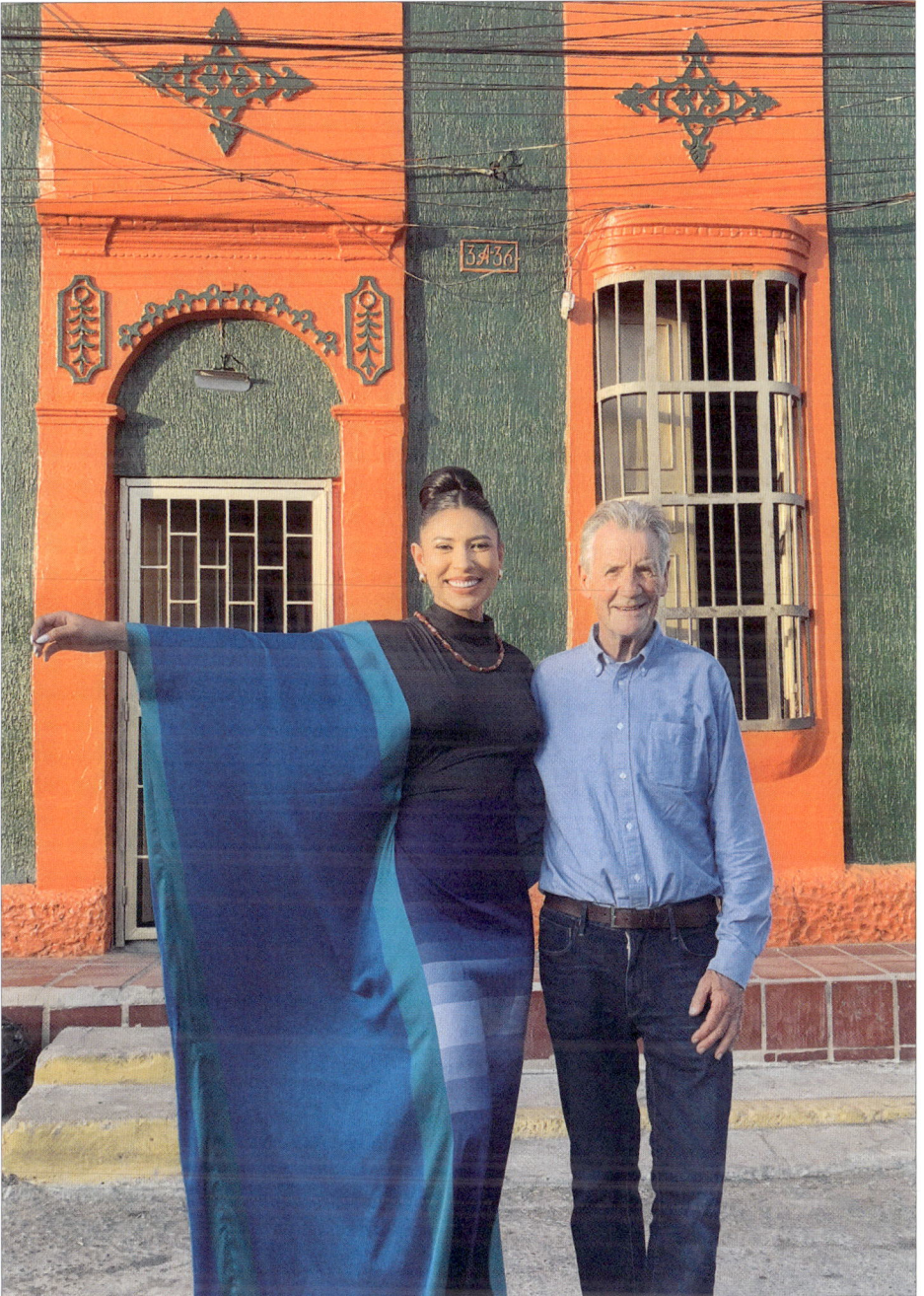

with a green trim. A young man, later revealed to be her make-up artist, walks attentively behind her.

She exudes composed confidence, but is far from lofty. From a very early age, she tells me, her ambition was to be a beauty queen. In many countries that goal would raise eyebrows. But in Venezuela it's viewed as the equivalent of aspiring to be a top athlete or tennis player. However, there is a price to pay, and as we talk I realise how much hard, often painful work she has had to put in to get where she is now. She freely admits to having had breast and face enhancements to improve her chances in the closely controlled arena of competitive beauty. Considerable resilience has been required to survive in what is a pretty unpleasant world.

Her openness is as surprising to me as her willingness to have so much work done, but she's not apologetic. Nor, it seems, is she easily ruffled. At one of the big contests she not only came second but in full view of the television cameras slipped and fell as she made her way off the stage. Yet she's able to laugh it off. It was good for business, in her view. Such moments, she adds, also help with her public visibility, ensuring that people are more likely to listen to her when she talks about more serious matters, such as the conditions endured by indigenous communities.

I walk with her in the streets around the Pa' Que Luis. The sun is setting, providing some relief from the heat and softening the bright colours of the houses around. People are beginning to arrive for the evening's entertainment. There'll be meeting and drinking and singing and doing the *gaita*, a mix of folk music and line-dancing which is a speciality of Zulia state.

We pass a church painted a rich blue, and spot, in the distance, the twin spires of one decorated in turquoise and white. What goes on there, and here in the bar on the corner, are the eternals of life in Maracaibo. Religion and music. Long before oil and long after.

Fierce winds are blowing off the lake tonight. Back in my room, I push the curtain aside but can see no lightning.

★DAY★
17

MARACAIBO TO MARACAY

IT'S STILL DARK WHEN WE LEAVE MARACAIBO. WE PASS
the National Guard barracks and the faces of Chávez and Maduro on a
big billboard opposite that also bears the legend *'Time for Leadership'*.

There are various combinations to be seen on these leadership
posters: Simón Bolívar and Hugo Chávez; Hugo Chávez and Nicolás
Maduro; sometimes Simón Bolívar and Hugo Chávez and the thin,
bespectacled figure of General Zamora who led a peasants' rebel-
lion in 1846. Simón Bolívar is, of course, the one Chávez championed.
Maduro, who was an ordinary party member when chosen to take over
after Chávez's death from cancer in 2013, has elevated himself to this
august company, visually identifying himself, through his appearance
at Chávez's side, with the ultimate Venezuelan hero – Simón Bolívar.

IN VENEZUELA

A security check at the entrance to the Maracaibo bridge, then out into the countryside. Roadside businesses are setting up. Fruit, *arepas, empanadas,* woven baskets, mats, hats, crucifixes.

On Highway 3 we join the queue at another *peaje,* and then head east into Falcon state. We're now well into carnival weekend, and the activity on the roads – along with the checkpoints – has increased correspondingly. Fortunately, the security police seem to have absorbed some of the carnival spirit. Surveillance seems more relaxed. There are more smiles than scowls.

About mid-morning we reach one of the oldest and most historic cities of Venezuela. Coro, founded in 1527, was the entry point for the Spanish colonisers and remained loyal to the Spanish crown well into the era of the independence movement of the early nineteenth century. It retains an eye-catching architectural legacy, its narrow streets full of colonial-style houses proving a draw for the crowds.

We don't linger in town because there is another unique piece of Venezuelan landscape to be seen just outside it: another national park, another completely distinctive feature, the Médanos de Coro – the Sands of Coro. Turn a corner beside a filling station and there it is. A body double for the Sahara. A sea of golden sand dunes stretching 35 square miles (90 square kilometres) to the coast. I struggle up to the top of one. Sinking into the Sands of Coro is bad enough but once at the top the lesser-known Winds of Coro catch me and for a moment it's hard to stand up. As ever, at moments when I feel myself marginally heroic for having got there at all, I'm upstaged. A party of about thirty small children scamper up to the top of an adjacent dune without a pause for breath.

The road to Maracay runs roughly parallel to the coast. It's thick with carnival traffic, and I find myself missing the clear air of the Andes and the wide open spaces of Los Llanos. There is a lot of unsettling human driftwood by the sides of the road – abandoned smallholdings, beachside properties started but never finished.

And then, out of nowhere, there rises a huge industrial plant: a refinery run by Pequiven (Petrochemicals of Venezuela), one of the giant nationalised industries set up in the Chávez years. Smoking, steaming and stained. It looks its age.

Another *peaje*, another queue. Into Aragua state, where our road journey started what seems like months ago.

We're back among the mountains as we approach Maracay, which vaunts itself as the Garden City and lives up to the name, with tree-lined avenues and a feeling of quiet self-confidence.

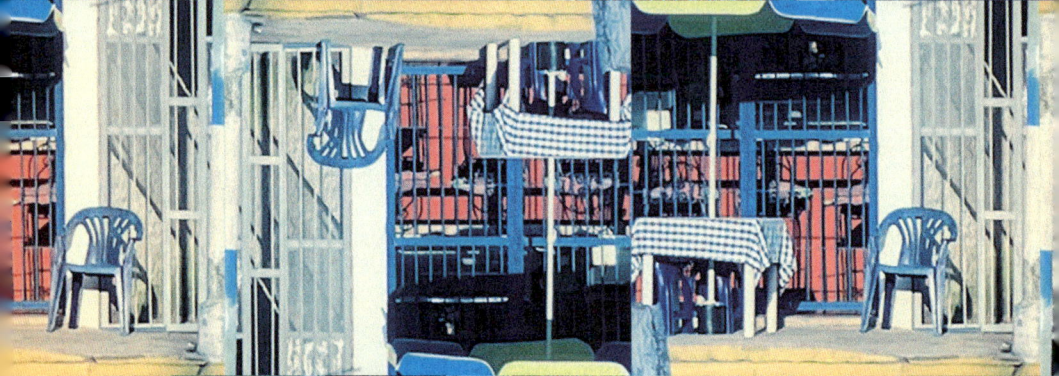

★DAY★
18

MARACAY TO CHUAO

INSTEAD OF TAKING THE MAIN ROAD OUT OF MARACAY
we are heading over the mountains to the coastal town of Choroni.
The route runs through the Henri Pittier National Park, named after
a Swiss geographer and botanist who studied and classified more than
thirty thousand plants in Venezuela. The oldest of the country's many
national parks, it encompasses yet another stretch of stunning scenery.

We travel on a narrow, twisting, two-lane road that climbs steeply
out of the valley and through forested slopes for the best part of an
hour. We pass many hikers, bikers and even walkers, but as the only
access to Choroni is via this road there are also trucks and vans and
buses grinding upwards or swaying perilously round the hairpin bends
on their way down.

It takes about two hours before we begin to see the first houses on the outskirts of Choroni. Some are comfortable-looking villas with high fences and verdant gardens. I'm told that many of these belong to people who have made money in Caracas but want a refuge away from city life.

A network of ever-narrowing streets, with attractive old house-fronts and stalls squeezing traffic almost to a standstill, brings us eventually to the beach. It's a hub of life this carnival weekend. The fishermen, whose boats and nets are stored here, have become marine taxi-drivers for the day, doing all they can to ferry holidaymakers to nearby beaches on what looks like a very choppy Caribbean.

Much as I'd like to stay and take in the colourful buzz of Choroni, we too are in transit, on our way to the village of Chuao, a little way up the coast, and accessible only by boat.

The fishing boats that take us are practical rather than comfortable and once we're pushed out onto the water it's a question of hanging on for dear life as we round a rocky headland and into a succession of alarmingly high waves that fling us up into the air and smack us down again. These being fishing boats and their occupants primarily fish, there is very little for humans to hang on to. And it's impossibly dangerous to film.

We bounce along for nearly half an hour until the engine pitch drops to a low rumble and we turn into a wide, sandy bay. It's been worth the wild ride. Chuao looks beautiful. Dozens of brightly painted fishing boats are drawn up on the shore and nets are drying on the concrete promenade.

It's tempting to assume that we're here so that we can admire the

village's beauty. In fact, we're visiting Chuao because this corner of paradise produces what some consider the purest chocolate in the world.

Elena, a warm and friendly Afro-Venezuelan wearing a vivid yellow-patterned dress and a matching headband, runs the business. She greets me, and with a big smile motions us all towards a well-worn, open-topped truck. She and the crew climb onto the back, but I'm afforded the luxury of a seat inside next to Wilfred, the laconic driver. The gear-stick is long with a polished black top. Not something you'd see at home outside a motor museum. Infinitely slowly we pull away from the waterfront and up the hill. The trees close in on either side and quite soon it feels as if we are in the heart of a lush tropical jungle.

After a few minutes' drive Elena asks Wilfred to pull up. She wants to show me the very beginning of the chocolate-making process. The cacao beans.

The cacao is a low, unremarkable tree from whose trunk hang bulbous pods the size of small rugby balls. Elena cracks one of them open on the side of the tree and shows me the tiny beans, encased in protective pulp. With a fine sense of drama, she extracts one of them and hands it carefully to me. And that is how I first experience the taste of the best chocolate in the world. Such is its value, I learn later, that it's illegal to remove a cacao pod from the tree unless you have the requisite licence.

It's a slight, subtle taste, but there is a hint of bitter intensity there which promises something special.

Back in the truck we make our way through the cacao plantation

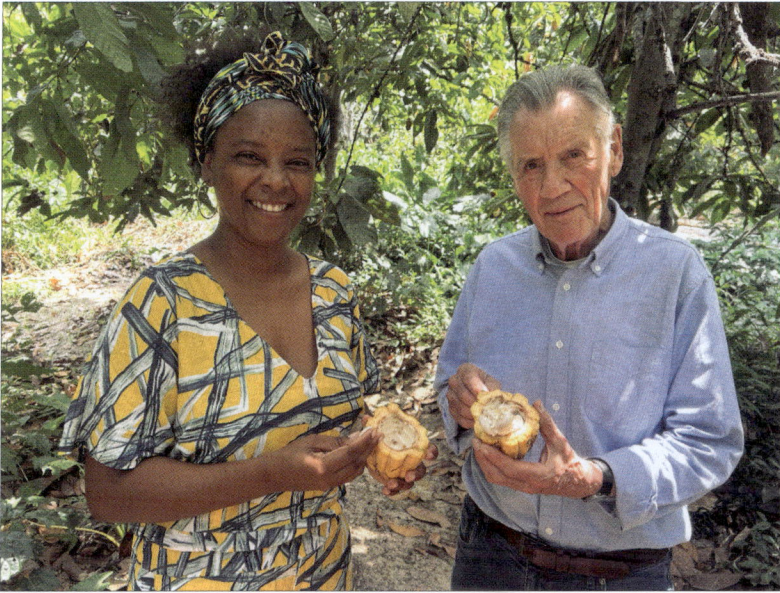

and into the village of Chuao itself. A huge painting of Jesus stands by the arched entrance, making it seem as though we're approaching a convent.

Once we're inside the village, dogs greet us with mild curiosity; otherwise everything's very quiet. That's because there's hardly a car to be seen. Three parallel streets of modest two-storey houses – many of them, I notice, named after saints – lead up to Chuao's only conspicuous building, a church painted light brown with a dark brown trim. Beyond it rise the mountains.

Chuao has around two thousand inhabitants, most of them descendants of slaves brought over from Africa by the Spanish colonisers to labour on plantations where almost anything would grow. Two hundred of the inhabitants work for the cocoa-producing Empresa Campesina Chuao company, which operates from a modest row of

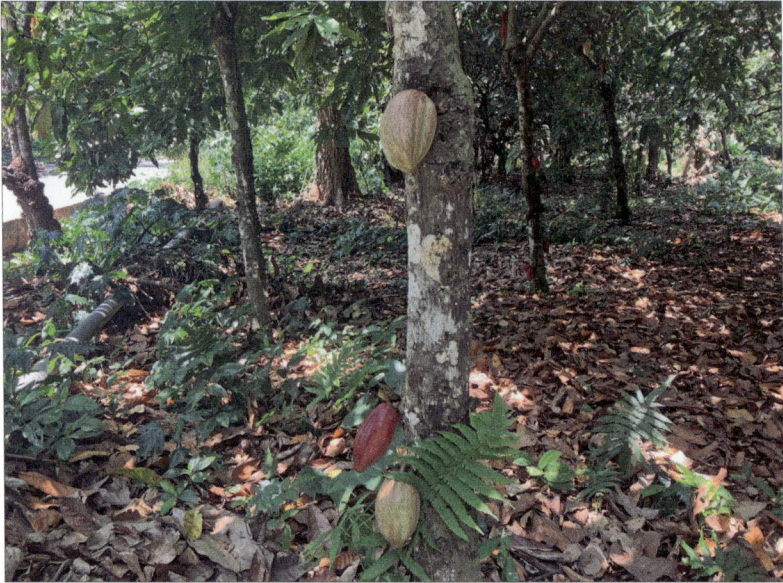

buildings next to the police station. Here rooms like stalls in a stable lead off a loggia supported by a row of elegant columns.

Elena takes me through the various processes involved in the preparation of cacao. First I'm led into a darkened room in which I can just make out wooden tanks and thick piles of leaves. This is the Fermentation Room, in which the cacao beans, still in their pulp, are covered with banana leaves for seven days to break down sugars and acids and intensify the flavour. Elena encourages me to reach into one of the tanks. I'm practically at arm's length before I make contact with a warm, pulpy, jelly-like mass below the leaves. Anything less like luxury chocolate I can't imagine.

Once they have been fermented, these pampered beans are then laid out to dry in the sun for another seven days. This step is not nearly as straightforward as it sounds. Both the temperature at which the

beans are dried and the kind of surface on which they're laid will affect the flavour of the final product. In front of the church there is an open area where the different drying surfaces – rough or smooth concrete, more or less heat-absorbent – on which the beans are laid can clearly be seen. Given the importance of chocolate and religion in this small town, it seems appropriate that the two should meet here.

The work is not entirely machine-free. After being dried, the beans are rotated manually in a handsomely antiquated metal drum made in Paris some time in the 1930s. As it is turned, different meshes filter the beans according to size. This, however, is not the end of the selection story, because there still remains what, for me, is the most engaging part of the process. This is undertaken manually by a group

of women sitting at a table on the shaded terrace. Here experience is everything, for the women have to rely on a highly developed sense of touch to pick out those beans that are of precisely the right size for maximum flavour. Making that very precise judgement is clearly a great skill, learnt over many years.

The sight of these women at work, singing to keep themselves going, is the single image that sums up why the beans that make the final cut go to make just about the world's finest chocolate.

Not that they have the facilities to make chocolate here. What the Empresa Campesina Chuao produces are the very best cacao beans from the very best environment in the world. It's up to individual importers to decide how to make use of them. These include high-end chocolatiers in France, Italy, the USA and – a little to my surprise – Scotland.

The company's business plan is explained to me by Mr Miyasaka, a middle-aged Japanese man who bankrolls the company in return for an exclusive contract for the sale of the beans. He pays $10 a kilo, which just about keeps things going. Two-thirds of his sales go to Europe; most of the balance to Japan.

Quality is so far ahead of quantity in this enterprise that Mr Miyasaka tells me, with some pride, that an entire year's production will fit into two of the fishing boats we took to get here.

Our visit to Empresa Campesina Chuao over, we set out for the Posada La Luzonera, a small, modest and cheerful hotel where we'll be spending the night. There are tables out front beneath lemon-and-blue umbrellas and a balcony above with a hammock and comfy chairs. I take advantage of one of the latter to have a peaceful afternoon nap.

As the day goes on, so do the preparations for Chuao's own carnival. Various events and displays are planned, among which – in another manifestation of the national obsession with beauty contests – will be the election of Chuao's own beauty queen.

In keeping with the unhurried lifestyle I've noticed here, the preparations drag on into the evening. Gradually, attendees, some disembarking from coaches, gather in front of the church. In the brightly lit front room of a house nearby, finishing touches are made to make-up and hair. It's well into night-time before everything and everyone is in place, the sound system is working properly and the

judges can take their seats at a long table decorated with white cotton gauze. Each has a bottle of Pepsi in front of them, the public consumption of alcohol being quite frowned on so close to the church, the doors of which have been screened with an orange-and-white backcloth. Above them the Virgin Mary is illuminated at a window.

The opening speeches are delivered and the show begins. It's much grander than I expected – some fifty or so dancers, young and old, in dazzling costumes, providing an energetic, well-drilled,

well-rehearsed song-and-dance overture. Later, the programme tells me, girls competing to be queen will have to appear first in bikini and then folk *gaita* outfits.

But by that time I've taken to my bed. We've had another long day and tomorrow we shall be back in Caracas, which I'm sure will host its own carnival processions for us to watch.

I was worried earlier about the potentially sleep-shattering noise of my air-con, but that turns out to be the least of my problems. As I lie down I can barely hear it over the noise of the carnival. Even so, I go on to enjoy one of the best night's sleep I've had since I arrived in Venezuela.

DAY 19

CHUAO TO CARACAS

IT'S HALF-PAST SEVEN IN THE MORNING AND I'M
looking out from the balcony of the *posada*. Complete silence has
replaced the raucousness of the night before. Streets have been swept
and the square by the church is empty again. There is no one on the
stone benches under the mango tree.

The clouds have cleared from the green-clad mountains. Wilfred
the driver nods a greeting as he passes on his way to get the truck ready
for our departure.

At breakfast – the Spanish classic *huevos revueltos*, scrambled
eggs with tomato, peppers and onions – we celebrate the birthday of big
José, my minder. He has always been a reassuring presence behind me,
particularly in the busy places. He's also presumed to be the number
one suspect as the Big Snorer in our night in the hammocks. Which
of course he denies. None of us presses the point. He is an ex-wrestler.

I feel a warm affection for this attractive, harmonious little town. After nearly three hectic weeks of trying to see and understand a country of which I knew so little, there's a feeling of having arrived at the end of the rainbow – of having reached somewhere which is, for once, not on the way to anywhere else.

Venezuela is a very beautiful country and yet there have been times when it has felt hostile, times when we've had to reach yet again for our passports, to explain yet again why we are here, and what our intentions might be.

But now, today, here in Chuao, I've experienced something quite untainted by the politics and the paranoia. There's a lack of complication in our relationship with the people here. We don't have to be on the defensive. Both the physical and mental pace of travel has momentarily slackened. Chuao is the one place where I've been able to put my

feet under the table, and for the first time since leaving London, I've felt at home.

This comforting interlude doesn't last long. We have to be back in Caracas by tonight. Chuao has not really woken up by the time we start to make our way back to the boat, through the cacao plantation, and across a thin river whose flow, Elena told me, has a mountain purity that is part of what makes her cacao beans so special.

The Caribbean is calmer today and the voyage back to Choroni more of a pleasure. This time around we are able to take in the striking beauty of the rocky coastline and the beaches tucked away at the bases of sheer cliffs.

Freddy's main interest, when he's not looking after groups like our own, is caving, and he tells us with great excitement that a previously unknown cave network has recently been found – quite by accident – among the coastal mountains we're currently sailing past. Apparently, researchers studying the nesting habits of oilbirds, locally known as *guacharos*, noticed that during the mating season these small, nocturnal birds seemed to disappear into the mountainside. When the researchers were eventually able to penetrate this very difficult terrain, they discovered that their destination was an elaborate and hitherto undiscovered cave system.

Choroni beach is livening up as carnival weekend visitors arrive. We're among the very few going in the opposite direction. We return to Maracay via the tortuous, unforgettably scenic road over the mountains and through the forest, before joining the *autopista* to Caracas. Just outside Maracay we pass what looks like an abandoned highway, raised on concrete supports and running several miles before petering out. Apparently this is a railway line, the only one we've seen in Venezuela. There seems to be nothing on it.

We reach a busy *peaje* some twelve miles from Caracas. Two large inflatable figures look down on us from the top of the gantry. One is the President of Venezuela dressed as Super Moustache, with red vest, little bulging muscles, dark glasses and tight blue trunks. The other, bobbing about in the breeze next to him, is his blonde wife, in a much inferior costume. It's a very surreal sight, and it leaves me wondering why a man tough enough to have clung to power for twelve years, running the country with the help of ruthless security forces for all that time, should feel the need to be portrayed as a slightly overweight Superman. Is it an attempt to portray himself as a folksy figure? A man who can take a joke? A leader who, after a minute or two in a phone box, can emerge to take on the world?

Or perhaps President Maduro, one of whose first moves after his disputed election was to bring Christmas forward to 1 October, sees carnival weekend as another celebratory diversion. Maybe that's why his inflatable adorns the *peaje* here at La Salinas.

I've noticed as we've travelled around that despite his chummy 'friend of the people' image, hardly any of the Venezuelans I've spoken to ever talk about him. It's as if there is a tacit understanding that the merest mention – of him, of his policies, even of politics in general – could land you in trouble. As for the overall situation in the country, a few people have been prepared to voice private complaints. But I have the strong impression that after the last grim decade there's no appetite for concerted opposition or upheaval. The general view seems to be that things are not actually getting worse, and that they could even possibly be getting slightly better, albeit from a low base. And that's sufficient. Venezuelans call this *tensa calma,* a tense calm.

The main Caracas Carnival has, for some reason, been moved to tomorrow, but there is a big procession promised at La Guaira just to the west of the city. Crowds are gathering on the beach and beside the road. Posters and billboards advertising the occasion all bear the words *'Supported by the office of President Maduro'*.

The La Guaira celebrations have all the hallmarks of government-sponsored fun, which makes me that much more grateful for having been present at the community-organised carnival in Chuao.

There's a lot of waiting around in the heat before the procession lumbers into view, led by a squadron of police on motorbikes. The floats themselves are fine, if a bit corporate, and disappointingly few in number. But there's much cheering and applause as they go slowly by and those on the floats throw sweets and squirt some white gunge on the crowds who have so patiently waited for them.

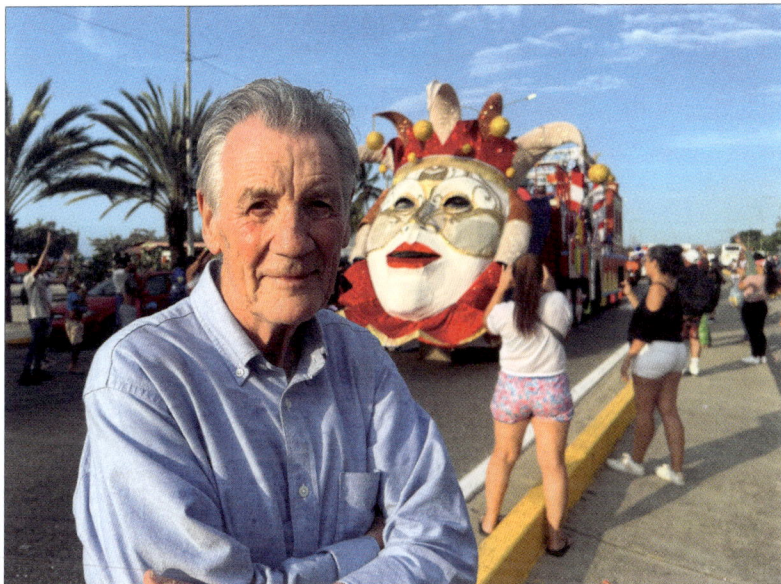

The heat and the crowds and the long slow drive back to the hotel in dense traffic are not made more bearable by rumours that our flight home tomorrow has been cancelled and that we will have to re-book for the next day. I wish it had all been different. Venezuela deserved a happier ending. But over a last Polar beer in the hotel bar, strangely empty as usual, we remember just how much we've seen and how the last three weeks have brought a striking and spectacular reality to a country none of us knew.

CARACAS TO ISTANBUL

IT SHOULD BE EASIER TO VISIT VENEZUELA. GLAD THOUGH we are of being able to catch a flight out today, it seems crazy that we have to go via Istanbul. It was not always like this. In the 1970s you could fly Concorde to the Venezuelan capital. Air France ran a five-times-weekly service, either supersonic or by the recently introduced 747s. The country was one of the most sought-after destinations in the world. This was the decade when the oil boom gave Venezuela the impressive road system that we saw so much of, and engineering wonders like the spectacular Humboldt hotel, and the world-beating *teleférico* in Mérida. A time when its schools and hospitals and universities were as good as any in the world.

Back then, Venezuelans went to Miami for a vacation. In the last decade, millions of Venezuelans have gone to Miami to escape economic collapse. So desperate have they been to leave the country of their birth that they have been prepared to negotiate the Darién Gap, one of the most hostile environments in the world, rather than face the hardships back home. (When we made *Full Circle*, my journey round the Pacific Rim, the Darién Gap was the one place we missed, so difficult and dangerous was it deemed to be.)

As we queue to check in at the airport this morning I look at the pattern on the mosaic tiles beneath my feet. It's characteristically Venezuelan: colourful, bold and bright. A fellow passenger tells me that those who choose to exile themselves from the country often point a camera to their feet on this distinctive tiled floor and then post the resulting photo online, to let others know that they have gone – and why they have gone.

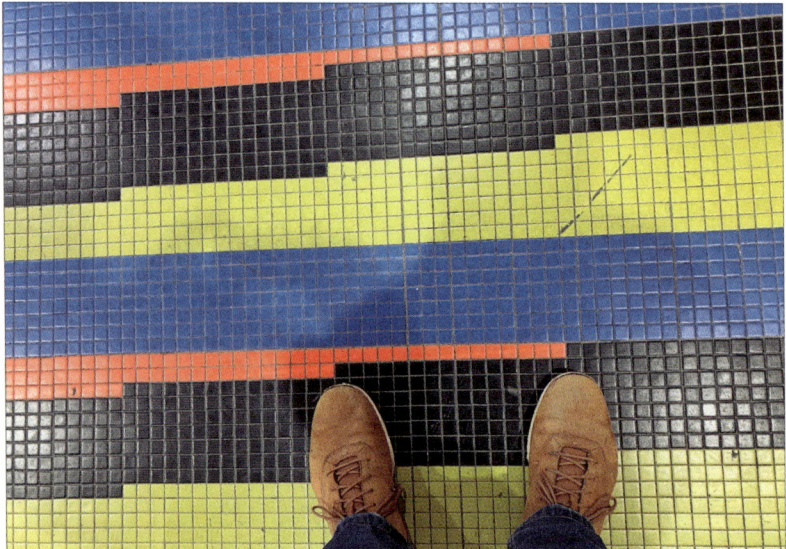

What seems like hours later we take off for Istanbul. As we bank to the north over the deep blue waters of the Caribbean, the steep green mountains recede and Venezuela becomes once again just a blur on the horizon. That seven million people should elect to leave such a unique country seems, on one level, inexplicable. But then that's the word that comes to mind when I try to comprehend Venezuela's current predicament. Inexplicable.

POSTSCRIPT

FOR MANY NIGHTS AFTER MY TRIPS ABROAD MY
dreams are full of images of where I've travelled and what I've seen.
Sometimes the images are so intense that I feel as though I've not yet
come home.

So it has been with Venezuela. And yet, there has also been something different this time. Muddled memories of standing on mountain
tops, huddling behind waterfalls and holding anacondas have crowded
my sleep, but once I have awoken each morning I have found it frus-
tratingly hard to distil from them an overall impression of the country
from which I have so recently returned.

I think much of the reason for this is Venezuela's sheer size and
scale – and its emptiness. It's a geographical giant compared to my
other recent destinations, yet it has far fewer inhabitants than Iraq or
Nigeria, and not that many more than North Korea.

So in my dreams it is a place of great beauty and of mysterious inaccessibility: a land of forests stretching off into the distance, of mountains towering over narrow winding roads, of rivers passing mile after mile of silent, uninhabited banks. To the north an abrupt coastline of rocky mountains plunging into the ocean; to the south vast forests stretching to limitless horizons. A country that seems to have no beginning and no end. A country, consequently, that to my waking brain is hard to define.

My daytime thoughts have also inevitably been coloured by the all-too-real news stories about the country, albeit ones delivered by a media currently more concerned with other parts of the world. A president determined to stay in power at all costs, his position apparently strengthened by victories in the latest state elections that are principally due to the opposition's tactically questionable refusal to go to the polls. Ugly scenes of Venezuelans being deported illegally from the USA and sent to a huge jail in El Salvador – a reminder of the price the country continues to pay for its particular brand of socialism.

I don't know where the future for Venezuela lies, but I know that there is great wealth hidden in those mountains and forests: gold and minerals and oil in abundance. There's another important commodity, too: the enterprise of the Venezuelan people. That, and their welcoming generosity, needs to be acknowledged by those in charge, and also flaunted to the rest of the world.

Then Venezuela could be a country of many people's dreams, not just mine.

MICHAEL PALIN　　　　　　　　　　　London, June 2025

CHRONOLOGY

c. 13,000 BCE   Early human settlement begins in the region now known as Venezuela

1498 CE   Christopher Columbus reaches Venezuela on his third voyage

1522   Spanish colonisation begins. Native tribes are subdued or convert to Roman Catholicism

1810   Beginning of the War of Independence against Spain

1821   Simón Bolívar secures independence for a large area of South America known as 'Gran Colombia', from which Venezuela secedes in 1830

1914   Oil discovered on the eastern shore of Lake Maracaibo

1945   Civilian government established after decades of military rule, but is overthrown in 1948 in a military coup led by Marcos Pérez Jiménez

1958   Establishment of democratic rule

1973   Election of Carlos Andrés Pérez as president, during whose first term in office Venezuela benefits from an international boom in oil prices

1983   Rise in public debt in the wake of falling oil prices and increased government expenditure leads to currency devaluation. Throughout the 1980s and '90s standards of living fall, levels of crime rise and civil unrest increases

1992 Colonel Hugo Chávez and supporters make two coup attempts

1993 Carlos Andrés Pérez, who began his second presidency in 1989, is forced from office on corruption charges

1998 Hugo Chávez elected president. He launches a 'Bolivarian Revolution', involving a new constitution and socialist and populist economic and social policies, funded by high oil prices

2001–7 During his second term as president, Chávez continues his socialist reforms and seeks closer relations with Russia and Cuba

2012 Despite a worsening economic situation, Chávez wins a fourth term in office

2013 Chávez dies. Nicolás Maduro, his chosen successor, is elected president by a narrow margin. Opposition parties dispute the result

2017 US imposes sanctions on Venezuela

2024 Maduro claims victory in contested presidential elections and begins his third term in office. Over the previous ten years living standards in Venezuela have declined by 74 per cent

ACKNOWLEDGEMENTS

ALONGSIDE NEIL FERGUSON, OTHERS WHO SHARED THE road with me were Jaimie Gramston on camera, Joe Morsman on sound, Alex Lobsang, assistant camera, and Matthew Archard, our medic.

The journey would not have been possible without our Venezuelan assistant producer Emiliana Ammirata. She helped prepare the series and, once on the road, her local knowledge, diligence and coolness under pressure saw us through many difficult moments.

I would also like to thank Guy Davies at Channel 5 and Ian Rumsey at ITN for all their support, and Will Smith for the benefits of his sage advice and experience.

Steve Abbott and Paul Bird at Mayday Management were enormously helpful throughout, and I must thank Mimi Robinson at Mayday for once again collating and transcribing my taped ramblings, and last, but very far from least, Nigel Wilcockson for being the perfect publisher once again.

HUTCHINSON HEINEMANN

UK | USA | Canada | Ireland | Australia
India | New Zealand | South Africa

Hutchinson Heinemann is part of the
Penguin Random House group of
companies whose addresses can be found
at global.penguinrandomhouse.com

Penguin Random House UK,
One Embassy Gardens, 8 Viaduct Gardens,
London SW11 7BW

penguin.co.uk

Penguin
Random House
UK

First published 2025
001

In Venezuela
Copyright © Michael Palin, 2025

Photographs are reproduced
by kind permission of:
Neil Ferguson pp. 8, 10, 11, 14, 16, 40–41, 43, 45,
48, 49, 50–51, 52, 53, 56, 57, 59, 60, 61, 64, 65, 71,
72 (bottom), 73, 74 (top), 75, 80 (top), 87, 88, 89,
116, 126, 151, 157, 160, 162, 163, 164–65;
Joe Morsman pp. 3, 19, 28, 32, 72 (top), 74
(bottom), 96, 100, 103, 108–9, 123, 128, 129, 147,
155, 168, 169, 172, 173;
Wikimedia Commons
(https://creativecommons.org/licenses)
pp. 78 (Marbe0506, CC BY-SA 3.0),
101 (Murray Foubister, CC BY-SA 2.0),
111 (George Miquilena, CC BY-SA 3.0),
135 (Orlando Pozo on Flickr, CC BY 2.0);
UCG via Getty Images p. 132.
All other photographs: Michael Palin.

Publisher: Nigel Wilcockson

Editorial assistant: Hannah White-Steele

Designer: Tim Barnes,
www.herechickychicky.com

Map: Darren Bennett,
www.dkbcreative.com

Printed and bound in Italy
by L.E.G.O. S.p.A

The authorised representative in the EEA is
Penguin Random House Ireland, Morrison
Chambers, 32 Nassau Street, Dublin D02 YH68

A CIP catalogue record for this book is
available from the British Library

ISBN: 978–1–529–15472–6